Federal Prison & Federal Prison Camp

A Beginner's Guidebook For First Time Inmates

About The Author:

Steve Vincent is considered by many to be America's Premier Federal Prison Consultant. Steve has helped hundreds of people prepare for Federal Prison and Federal Prison Camp with his professional, unique and caring program that is designed to do one thing, get you prepared for prison without scaring or embarrassing you. Steve teaches what you need to know in order to stay safe during your period of incarceration with a positive message that places emphases on you surviving, improving yourself during the time and realizing that you will be going home. This is the same guidebook that Steve uses in his private sessions with his clients.

This guidebook does not provide, suggest offering, or implying to give, any legal advice of any kind. If you need any legal questions answered, we suggest you call an attorney.

KY PUBLISHING'S

Federal Prison & Federal Prison Camp – A Beginner's Guidebook for First Time Inmates

© KY Publishing
2326 Winston Ave.
Louisville, Ky 40205

ISBN: 978-0-6151-8506-4

Table of Contents

Introduction

Make the best use of what is in your power, and take the rest as it happens.
Epictetus (55 AD - 135 AD)

The purpose of this guidebook is to provide general information about what an inmate's daily life is like at low security prisons and prison camps. It is information that will aid you in adjusting to the routine of life as an inmate. While no two prisons are exactly the same, and regardless if you are a man or a woman, the day-to-day life of their inmates is quite similar.

Prisons - Protecting Society

Prisons are built and designed to be places that house offenders in controlled environments. The Federal Bureau of Prisons (BOP), and most states, will tell you that their prisons are safe, humane, cost-efficient, and appropriately secure. They provide work and other self-improvement opportunities to assist offenders in becoming law-abiding citizens.

As of January 4th, 2007 the Federal Bureau of Prisons reported that there were a total of 193,173 inmates currently being housed in their institutions across the United States. Between 1973 and 2000 the rate of incarceration in the United States more than quadrupled. The Federal Bureau of Justice Statistics reports that at the end of 2005, there were 2,193,798 prisoners being held in Federal or State Prisons or in local jails. What this all means is that the United States has a higher percentage of the population in prison than any other nation on earth. It's been said that in your lifetime, you, someone in your family, or someone that you know will serve time in prison. The "Get Tough on Crime" approach to criminal justice that America adopted has caused overcrowded prisons with deteriorating structures. It's these conditions that greatly contribute to prisoner violence. The prison system is always one department, of both Federal and State Governments, which can almost be guaranteed to receive budget cuts each year.

> *"For the vast majority of inmates prison is a temporary, not a final, destination. The experiences inmates have in prison — whether violent or redemptive — do not stay within prison walls, but spill over into the rest of society. Federal, state, and local governments must address the problems faced by their respective institutions and develop tangible and attainable solutions."*
> *—**Senator Tom Coburn** (R-OK), Chair, Senate Judiciary Subcommittee on Corrections and Rehabilitation*

Now that you know that prisons are very overcrowded, under funded, and generally structurally falling apart, we will begin to get you prepared for going.

Freedom

The very idea of having our freedom taken away from us goes against everything that we, as Americans, were brought up to believe in. Being locked away from your family and friends for a period of months or years can be very stressful. This traumatic time in your life doesn't only affect you; it can also have a devastating impact on your family. Ask any former inmate and they will tell you that while they were incarcerated it was their family that suffered the most. If you are in the position of having family members who are worried about you're pending incarceration at a prison or prison camp, please encourage them to also read this guidebook. We have discovered that once a person has a better understanding of what being an inmate is really like; it helps them to deal with the situation much better.

Hollywood

The majority of people gain all of their knowledge about prison by watching Hollywood movies and television shows. While some of what those movies and TV shows portray is close to being accurate, we believe you will be surprised at how much they get wrong. Prison can be physically hard sometimes and, as you will soon discover, it will be a major change in lifestyle for you, which probably won't be easy. But prison is mostly mentally challenging and, once you get adjusted, you will realize that they are nothing more than daycare centers that are run like military boot camps for angry adults who are always standing in line and who often act like children. Sometimes you will feel like a child. You will be fed, told when to go to bed each night and when to wake each morning. You will be given orders and you will be yelled and screamed at.

Prison is also all about routine. Activities will always be at the exact same time each day and inmates will do everything the exact same way. No individualism is allowed in prison. Most inmates will tell you that the longer you stay the easier it gets. I'm not sure I agree with that statement, but I will say that the longer you stay the more boring it gets.

- Read this guidebook several times.
- Encourage your family members to also read this guidebook.

Conduct

The Prison Staff will expect you to conduct yourself in a responsible manner at all times, to be courteous to others, to be respectful toward all, and to obey instructions immediately, with no questions asked. You will be responsible for strictly adhering to the rules and regulations. Serious offenses such as the introduction and/or possession of alcohol, marijuana, or other unauthorized drugs and aggressive behavior will normally constitute a transfer to an institution of greater security and supervision.

Violence, Violence, Violence

You purchased this guidebook because this will be your first prison experience and, like every first time inmate, you are probably nervous and scared about what may happen to you once you arrive at prison. The Hollywood movies and TV shows depict prison to be nothing but violence, violence, and more violence. The simple truth is the higher the level of security institution you go to the higher level of violent inmates you will find. All inmates know that the higher you go the more restrictions you will have. The higher you go the less freedom of movement you will have. The higher you go the more locked down you will be. The higher you go the more supervision you will get. The higher you go the tougher the guards. The higher you go the greater the chance of violence. The higher you go the longer you usually stay.

As mentioned above, all inmates at low security prisons and camps know that an act of violence could get them transferred up the ladder to the next level of security institution. No inmate wants to trade a low security prison for a medium, and only an idiot would trade a camp for a low. It's every inmate's goal to move down the ladder.

This is not to say that there aren't any fights or violent inmates at lows, because there are. But considering most lows usually house well over 1000 inmates, I would guess the percentage of fights and acts of violence are very low for that amount of men. There will always be those inmates who snap and may become violent. The stress level of being incarcerated away from your family and friends is very high. This guidebook will give you advice on how to avoid being in a situation that could lead to violence.

When inmates fight it's usually because of one of the 8 Sins of Prison. If it's your intention to do your time as quietly and stress free as possible, the chapters on the "8 Sins of Prison" and "The Inmate's 10 Commandments" will tell you what to stay away from and what not to do.

Fighting At Camps

Fighting at camps is very rare. Camps are designated to house non-violent inmates. Yes, I have seen a few fights at camp but they were more like what you would see in high school instead of what you may have seen in the prison movies. Federal Camps are often called Club Fed. They are, without a doubt, the most desirable places to serve time at, but they are still prisons. However, you will be surprised to find that camps operate with a minimum of rules and regulations. You will find considerable freedom of movement and less direct supervision that you might normally expect.

Hell-On-Earth

Prison can be a hell-on-earth if you allow it to be. If you don't keep your mind and body busy and you just sit around thinking about your situation it will be. There are thousands of negatives associated with being incarcerated and it would take volumes of books to list them. But prison can also be a healthy life changing experience for you. If you are overweight and have health problems because of it, you will have the opportunity to start an exercise program that you won't be able to say that you don't have the time to do. I have seen inmates who have lost well over 100 lbs in prison, and I personally lost over 75 lbs. Most prisons have a few cardio machines to workout on and a weight room for strength training. But even if you don't do anything else but walk each day, which a great number of inmates do, you will be surprised at how much weight you will lose. You will also find basketball, volleyball, billiards, handball, and some institutions have softball.

GED Program

There is also the chance to improve educationally. Almost all prisons have a GED program that is required if you didn't finish school. The prison's Educational Department will also offer classes on different things, like starting your own business and money management. There are some institutions that offer a class on getting a CCL License (Big Truck Driving). All prisons have a library that usually has a wide variety of books and magazines on different topics. Read, read, and then read some more.

TV & Music

All Federal Institutions have some type of Television Room, which usually has more than one TV. The TV's have basic cable and get quite a few channels. Usually there is one designated just for sports and one for movies. Federal Prisons also show DVD movies on weekends and holidays. These movies are rented from a local Blockbuster or other DVD rental store and usually are new releases.

Religion

Prisons are also a place for you to gain spiritually. Almost every religious belief is represented and if your religion isn't, they will provide what you need so it can be. There will be a Prison Chaplin that inmates can visit with, and outside religious leaders who volunteer their time to come in and have services throughout the week.

Good Friends

You will also find that you will make some good friends in prison. Believe me; nothing brings people closer then spending time in prison together. You will find that no matter how bad you believe your life is right now there will be a few inmates who have it worse. I have found that most inmates will do anything they can to help another inmate. When a new inmate arrives someone will usually loan him an old pair of shower shoes and give him a bar of soap. It doesn't sound like much but when you arrive at prison you will better understand the value of those items.

You will also find some of the biggest liars that God put on this earth in prison. There are more millionaires in the prison system then on Wall Street. One thing you have to remember is that 90% of everything you hear in prison is total B.S. But also know that the only thing you have as an inmate is your word. Keep it strong and you will be respected.

I know that this time in you life is filled with regret and depression. You are no different than any other inmate. We all must live with our poor choices we made that led us to prison. But also know this, one day this will all be behind you. Time continues to turn while you are in prison and from your first day inside the clock will start ticking off your sentence. It may seem overwhelming to you right now but you will get through it.

Everyday in prison should be a learning experience for you. I encourage you to take advantage of the many opportunities for self-improvement while you are there. Prison sucks, and that's the bottom line, but make the time serve you rather than you just serving the time. You can lose the time or use it to improve your body, mind, and spirit.

What Happens On Your First Day

It's the day you have been dreading. It's the day that you arrive at prison or camp to start serving your sentence. Regardless if you arrive by prisoner transport, bus, or if your family is dropping you off, nothing that I can say to you will describe what you will be feeling when you first get a look at those walls, fences and razor wire. Seeing them in a Hollywood movie or on television just doesn't accurately portray how imposing they really are. If you are serving your sentence at a federal camp you probably won't see any walls or fences. Though there are some that do have them, most state and federal camps are open areas that seem more like a college campus then a prison.

Your first day inside will consist of searches, fingerprinting, being photographed and possibly being thrown in the Hole (locked down segregation cell). Keep your questions to yourself during this process. The CO (Correctional Officer) doesn't want to answer questions. Questions are for the prison's counselors to answer. All the Receiving CO wants to do is get you processed in as quickly and quietly as possible. Don't begin serving your time by being labeled as a smartass by the CO's. Answer any and all questions he asks but otherwise keep quiet. Don't be surprised to find yourself handcuffed while you are being walked to and from different areas. In most institutions it is standard procedure. If you have never been handcuffed before (some self-surrenders haven't been), here is a tip for you. When told to place your hands behind your back, turn your knuckles toward each other with your thumbs up.

Once you arrive at prison you are on the prison staff's schedule. If the prisons medical staff, counselors or administrative personnel do not have the time to see you when you first arrive then you will be placed in a locked down cell (the Hole) until their schedule permits. Waiting to be processed in could take days or even weeks depending on the institution. You will not be assigned a cell or cube in a housing unit until it has been determined by the staff that by doing so will not place you in any obvious danger because of you having cooperated with the prosecution of another inmate or any other reason that could get you injured or possibly killed. If this is the case, which is rare, you will probably be housed in a segregated housing unit (the Hole). Unless you're prior history has law enforcement background or if you have given testimony in a well known case in the media or involving inmate(s) already housed at the institution, you should plan on going to general population. The institution will not place you in a segregated housing unit just because you are scared of what may happen to you in general population without a very compelling reason. They simply don't have the space.

Inmate Network

Be aware that inmates transfer from institution to institution on a regular basis. A lot of times they are transferred by the BOP (Bureau of Prisons) for their own protection because they have informed on other inmates at their previous stop. You will find that it doesn't take long before the news of what happened at their last place catches up to them at their new location. Inmates have that kind of network.

TB

You will also be seen at some point by the medical staff for a TB (tuberculosis test). This is usually given soon after you arrive and before you are allowed into general population. You will be scheduled for a full physical exam at a later date.

R&D

The fingerprinting and photograph is pretty standard stuff. They will probably take the digital copies of your fingerprints, as well as the old-fashioned ink copies. The photograph will be for your Prison ID & Commissary card as well as your jacket (file). The search is another matter. If you are already in custody then you know what to expect. If you are new to the system and have never had the "pleasure" of a full body cavity search then you are in for a new experience.

The R&D (Receiving & Discharge) CO will strip you down and make you spread and open any and all body cavities. Do not be stupid and attempt to smuggle something in with you. The CO has been highly trained and usually has a lot of experience doing the searches. They know what and where to look for contraband. If you are discovered attempting to smuggle contraband into a prison, you will be charged with a new crime. Your goal is to get through the time that you are there to serve without adding a single extra second to it. I know if you are facing a few years you might think what difference does another 12 months make? Trust me when I say that it will make a huge difference when you begin serving the extra 12 months. Some institutions will sit you in an x-ray chair to search even more thoroughly for concealed contraband or weapons, and don't be surprised if the CO snaps on a pair of medical gloves for a "deeper" search.

Lost and Lonely

Your first day inside will probably find you being scared, lost and lonely. Everyone has seen the prison movies or has heard stories about violent inmates. Most every first time inmate is scared of doing something wrong and scared of possibly being beaten or abused by other inmates. Every new inmate wants to fit in and be accepted by the other inmates as quickly as possible, but you should avoid being over friendly and too eager to make new friends. You will watch most everyone as most everyone will be watching you. At low and minimum prisons there is nothing wrong with making eye contact with other inmates, but don't stare. Staring is considered to be a hostile act by most inmates at all levels of prisons and will result in, at the very least, a verbal challenge. But be warned! The higher security institutions house the more violent inmates. Unless you are a gangbanger or just enjoy violence then you should use extreme caution around inmates at these higher security level prisons.

First time inmates always get watched by the other inmates. They are mostly sizing you up and wondering why you are there, but some are wondering if you will be an easy mark for them to take advantage of. Some inmates, for a type of recreation, may say things to new inmates just to see what kind of reaction they get. My advice to you is to answer a question if asked and ignore an insult if given. Be yourself! Don't try and be something that you are not just to try and impress the other inmates. They will see right through you. Bragging and talking like you are some big important person in the real world might also get you called out. Most inmates are broke and upon their release will have no homes to go back to. They don't want to listen to you telling everyone how many millions you have in the bank and about how many rooms your mansion has. They know you are probably lying and will soon get tired of hearing it. But regardless if you really do have several million in the bank and some super model waiting for you at home, just keep it to yourself, especially the part about the several million in the bank.

Like The Military

Prison, much like the military, is a very structured environment that has a right way and a wrong way of doing things. There is no middle ground. Most first timers will want to do everything the same way as the other inmates. Watching what other inmates do is natural and I would encourage it. They have been there long enough to know what the guards will tolerate, and what they won't. When you first arrived you should have been given some type of abbreviated rules and regulations manual by someone from the prison's staff. Take some time to read it and get to know what some of the policies and rules are. Most of these manuals only cover the very basics of rules and regulations, and you will soon discover that there are a few hundred that you will be expected to know and follow. The prison's library should have a copy of the complete rules and regulations manual or manuals. Take the time to look over them as soon as you can. You don't want to go to the Hole because you didn't know what the policies and rules were.

You will be issued bedding and, if the laundry is open, clothing. You also will be given a welcome package usually consisting of a small toothbrush, toothpaste or powder, razor, soap and a comb. This package will get you through until you can buy better supplies at the commissary.

Your Cell or Cube

Once you have been escorted to, or found your cell or cube, you will need to make up your bunk or bed. Again, the prison will follow military regulations when it comes to making your bunk. This means, as in boot camp, folded corners and tight fitting sheets and blankets with the folded back 4-inch collar. Just picture a drill sergeant bouncing a quarter off of you mattress and you will get the right idea. You should plan on sleeping on the top bunk of the bunk beds. Bottom bunks are assigned to inmates who are over 50 years of age, medically unable to climb up to the top bed, or those inmates with seniority.

Pillows are, depending on the institution, issued with your bedding or they are supposed to already be on your bunk. Some institutions are going with the foam mattress with the pillow built-in. I have heard that these type mattresses are small and very uncomfortable. If your pillow is not issued with your bedding there is a 100% chance, especially in a camp, that it won't be on your bunk. Most institutional pillows are about the size of a folded towel and other inmates consider having two a luxury. If you have a good celly or bunky they will ask around if someone has an extra pillow. In some cases it's your celly or bunky that has it and they will give it back to you. In most cases no one knows where you pillow is. At a camp it is okay to go to the laundry or CO and ask if you can be issued a pillow. They know that pillows often disappear from a vacant bunk and will usually make an announcement that, unless the pillow quickly reappears, there will be a shakedown to find it, and the inmate who has the extra pillow will be sent to the hole. In most cases the missing pillow will turn up. Though you don't ever want to appear to be a snitch or a whiner by going to the CO for anything, most inmates, not all, will let this pass because they expect you to ask for a pillow. However, be warned that if the pillow doesn't appear and a shakedown occurs, the CO will confiscate any contraband he can find from any locker he searches just because he is angry that he has to take the time to look for your pillow. You will be looked at by most inmates as the cause for any loss of their property. No shakedown ever occurs without the CO confiscating something.

With your bed made you should pack away your issued clothing in your locker. Almost all institutions have some form of small metal or wooden lockers for the inmates in their cells or cubes. In most cases you will be expected to purchase your own combination lock from the commissary, and I would recommend purchasing one as soon as possible. Until you can purchase a lock don't place anything in your locker that you would consider valuable. Having anything of real value in prison is highly unlikely, but I have heard of underwear being stolen from unlocked lockers. The general rule in prison is, don't have any possession that means so much to you that if it gets stolen you will do something to jeopardize your safety, or the remaining amount of time you have left to serve, to get it back.

Writing your name or number on your non-uniform clothing items (t-shirts, underwear, socks etc.) in magic marker, as soon as possible, is also a good idea. You can ask you're celly if he has a marker you can borrow to do this. Chances are if he has been at the institution for some time he will have one, or will know who does. Be advised that having a lock on your locker is no guarantee that someone won't be able to break into it. Also know that the CO's carry a master key that fits all of the combination locks. This allows them access to the lockers during a shakedown, or at any time they chose to do so. Your locker will be your combination clothes closet, food pantry and medicine chest. It will get searched on a regular basis so be prepared for that. You don't want to store anything in there that you don't want the CO's to find, because eventually they will find it.

Contraband

Contraband in prison is a no-no, but every inmate has some form of contraband. Some inmates have just an extra pair of socks, but some have drugs, weapons and cell phones. Some CO's will let the smaller things pass and some won't. It won't take long to learn which CO's will and which CO's won't. Most times possessing contraband will only get you a shot (written incident report) but, depending on what the contraband is, it may get you a trip to the hole, or a transfer to a more secure institution. If you take the chance and decide to hide contraband then realize that you probably aren't the first inmate to use that particular place to hide things. CO's are trained to know where to look for contraband. They have seen it all before. The only one to blame for you getting caught with contraband is you. Again, your goal is to get through the time that you are there to serve, and not add a single extra second to it or get any of your Good Time days taken away. Don't be stupid!

Depending on the security level of your institution, and the time of the move, your celly should give you a tour of the grounds. You should learn where the cafeteria, library, gym, chapel and other buildings are located. In addition learn where the out-of-bound areas are. Also be very sure of when the counts are made. You do not want to "screw up" a count by not being where you are supposed to be. The counts are sacred, and nothing makes the CO's madder than someone screwing up a count. Shots and the Hole is a 100% guarantee if you screw up the count.

Most first time inmates want to stay close to their cells or cubes when the first arrive. Unless you have friends that are serving time at your institution, and are allowed to leave your housing unit to visit with them in the yard, staying around your house is a good idea. Remember that being in any other housing unit beside your own is a no-no. Do your visiting where and when it is allowed. At most institutions the Block CO will not allow anyone in the unit who doesn't live there. Get caught trying and get a trip to the Hole for your effort. In camps the housing units won't have Block CO's and, while it is still a no-no, you can visit in other units. But be warned that if a CO does catch you in a unit that you don't live in, you will receive a shot and possibly a trip to the Hole. There is also a matter of things coming up missing in housing units, which usually always get blamed on inmates from other housing units that were seen visiting in the unit. Regardless if you know anything about the missing property or not, your name will be attached to the incident, and you will be labeled a possible sneak thief by the other inmates and the CO's.

What Can You Bring With You

Not Much

I will use the words "probably" and "should be" a lot in this chapter. This is one topic that you cannot be 100% positive about until you actually arrive.

The simple truth is that you can bring very little with you. If you are already in custody at a county jail, or some other facility you probably already have all that you are going to be able to bring into a prison or a camp. If you are lucky enough to be a self-surrender, who has been given a date and time to report to a camp or low security institution, then you should call ahead to find out for sure what is allowed. I would call at least 2 weeks ahead of your schedule time to arrive.

Call Them

Call the institution's main telephone number and ask to speak to a receiving CO or a counselor. When you speak to them ask what is allowed for an inmate to bring with them, when they arrive to self-surrender. In most cases you will be told nothing is allowed but in actuality you probably will be allowed a few items. Some institutions may be able to mail or fax you a list of items that are allowed. The following is a list of every Federal Prison in America:

FEDERAL CORRECTIONAL FACILITIES (U.S. FEDERAL BUREAU OF PRISONS)

Alabama Federal Prisons

FPC - Montgomery
Maxwell Air Force Base
Montgomery, AL 36112
334-293-2100
Fax: 334-293-2274

FCI - Talladega
565 East Renfroe Road
Talladega, AL 35160
205-362-0410
Fax: 205-315-4495

Arizona Federal Prisons

FCI - Phoenix
37900 North 45th Avenue
Department 1680
Phoenix, AZ 85027-7003
602-465-9757
Fax: 602-465-5133

FCI - Safford
RR 2, Box 820
Safford, AZ 85546-9729
602-428-6600
Fax: 602-348-1331

FCI - Tucson
8901 South Wilmot Road
Tucson, AZ 85706
520-574-7100
Fax: 520-670-5674

Arkansas Federal Prisons

FCI - Forrest City
PO Box 7000
Forrest City, AR 72335
870-630-6000
Fax: 870-630-6250

California Federal Prisons

FPC - Boron
PO Box 500
Boron, CA 93596
619-762-6230
Fax: 619-762-5719

FCI - Dublin
8th Street - Camp Parks
Dublin, CA 94568
510-833-7500
Fax: 510-833-7599

USP - Lompoc
3901 Klein Boulevard
Lompoc, CA 93436
805-735-2771
Fax: 805-737-0295

FCI - Lompoc
3600 Guard Road
Lompoc, CA 93436
805-736-4154
Fax: 805-736-7163

MDC - Los Angeles
535 North Alameda Street
Los Angeles, CA 90012
213-485-0439
Fax: 213-626-5801

MCC - San Diego
808 Union Street
San Diego, CA 92101-6078
619-232-4311
Fax: 619-595-0390

FCI - Terminal Island
1299 Seaside Avenue
Terminal Island, CA 90731
310-831-8961
Fax: 310-732-5335

Colorado Federal Prisons

ADX - Florence
PO Box 8500
Florence, CO 81226
719-784-9464
Fax: 719-784-5290

FCI - Florence
PO Box 6500
Florence, CO 81226
719-784-9100
Fax: 719-784-9504

USP - Florence
PO Box 7500
Florence, CO 81226
719-784-9454
Fax: 719-784-5157

FCI - Englewood
9595 West Quincy Avenue
Littleton, CO 80123
303-985-1566
Fax: 303-763-2553

Connecticut Federal Prisons

FCI - Danbury
Route 37
Danbury, CT 06811-3099
203-743-6471
Fax: 203-312-3110

Florida Federal Prisons

FCI - Coleman (Low)
868 NE 54th Terrace
Coleman, FL 33521-8999
352-330-3100
Fax: 352-330-0259FCI

FCI - Coleman (Medium)
811 NE 54th Terrace
Coleman, FL 33521-8997
352-330-3200
Fax: 352-330-0552

FPC - Eglin (closed 2006)
Eglin Air Force Base
PO Box 600
Eglin, FL 32542-7606
850-882-8552
Fax: 850-729-8261

FCI - Marianna
3625 FCI Road
Marianna, FL 32446
850-526-2313
Fax: 850-482-6837

FCI - Miami
15801 SW 137th Avenue
Miami, Florida 33177
305-259-2100
Fax: 305-259-2160

FDC - Miami
PO Box 0119118
33 Northwest 4th Street
Miami, FL 33101-9118
305-982-1114
Fax: 305-982-1357

FPC - Pensacola
110 Raby Avenue
Pensacola, FL 32509-5127
850-457-1911
Fax: 850-458-7295

FCI - Tallahassee
501 Capital Circle NE
Tallahassee, FL 32301-3572
904-878-2173
Fax: 904-216-1299

Georgia Federal Prisons

USP - Atlanta
601 McDonough Blvd. SE
Atlanta, GA 30315-0182
404-635-5100
Fax: 404-331-2137

FCI - Jesup
2600 Highway 301 South
Jesup, Georgia 31599
912-427-0870
Fax: 912-427-1125

Illinois Federal Prisons

MCC - Chicago
71 West Van Buren
Chicago, IL 60605
312-322-0567
Fax: 312-322-0565

FCI - Greenville
PO Box 4000
100 US Route 40
Greenville, IL 62246
618-664-6200
Fax: 618-664-6398

USP - Marion
Route 5, PO Box 2000
Marion, IL 62959
618-964-1441
Fax: 618-964-1695

FCI - Pekin
PO Box 7000
Pekin, IL 61555-7000
309-346-8588
Fax: 309-477-4688

Indiana Federal Prisons

USP - Terre Haute
Highway 63 South
Terre Haute, IN 47808
812-238-1531
Fax: 812-238-9873

Kansas Federal Prisons

USP - Leavenworth
1300 Metropolitan
Leavenworth, KS 66048
913-682-8700
Fax: 913-682-0041

Kentucky Federal Prisons

FCI - Ashland
PO Box 888
Ashland, KY 41105-0888
606-928-6414
Fax: 700-358-8552

FMC - Lexington
3301 Leestown Road
Lexington, KY 40511
606-255-6812
Fax: 606-253-8821

FCI - Manchester
PO Box 3000
Manchester, KY 40962
606-598-1900
Fax: 606-599-4115

Louisiana Federal Prisons

FCI - Oakdale
PO Box 5050
Oakdale, LA 71463
318-335-4070
Fax: 318-335-3936

FDC - Oakdale
P.O. Box 5060
Oakdale, LA 71463
318-335-4466
Fax: 318-335-4476

USP - Pollock
855 Airbase Road, #1
Pollock, LA 71467
318-765-0007
Fax: 318-765-2209

Maryland Federal Prisons

FCI - Cumberland
14601 Burbridge Road SE
Cumberland, MD 21502-8771
301-784-1000
Fax: 301-784-1008

Massachusetts Federal Prisons

FMC/FPC - Devens
42 Patton Road
Devens, MA 01432
978-796-1000
Fax: 978-796-1118

Michigan Federal Prisons

FCI - Milan
P.O. Box 9999
Arkona Road
Milan, Michigan 48160
734-439-1511
Fax: 734-439-0949

Minnesota Federal Prisons

FPC - Duluth
PO Box 1400
Stebner Road
Duluth, MN 55814
218-722-8634
Fax: 218-733-4701

FMC - Rochester
PO Box 4600
2110 East Center Street
Rochester, MN 55903-4600
507-287-0674
Fax: 507-287-9601

FCI - Sandstone
Kettle River Road
Sandstone, MN 55072
320-245-2262
Fax: 320-245-0385

FCI - Waseca
PO Box 1731
University Drive SW
Waseca, MN 56093
507-835-8972
Fax: 507-837-4558

Mississippi Federal Prisons

FCI Yazoo City
PO Box 5050
Yazoo City, MS 39194
601-751-4800
Fax: 601-751-4905

Missouri Federal Prisons

MCFP - Springfield

PO Box 4000
1900 West Sunshine
Springfield, MO 65801-4000
417-862-7041
Fax: 417-837-1711

Nevada Federal Prisons

FPC - Nellis (Closed 2006)

CS 4500
North Las Vegas, NV 89036-4500
702-644-5001
Fax: 702-644-7282

New Jersey Federal Prisons

FCI - Fairton

PO Box 280
Fairton, NJ 08320
609-453-1177
Fax: 609-453-4015

FCI/FPC - Fort Dix

PO Box 38
Fort Dix, New Jersey 08640
609-723-1100
Fax: 609-724-6847

New Mexico Federal Prisons

FCI - La Tuna
PO Box 1000
8500 Doniphan
Anthony, New Mexico-Texas 88021
915-886-3422
Fax: 915-886-4977

New York Federal Prisons

MDC - Brooklyn
100 29th Street
Brooklyn, NY 11232
718-832-1039
Fax: 718-832-4225

MCC - New York
150 Park Row
New York, NY 10007
212-240-9656
Fax: 212-417-7673

FCI - Otisville
P.O. Box 600
Otisville, NY 10963
845-386-5855
Fax: 914-386-9455

FCI - Ray Brook
PO Box 300
Ray Brook, NY 12977
518-891-5400
Fax: 518-891-0011

North Carolina Federal Prisons

FCI - Butner (Low)
PO Box 999
Butner, NC 27509
919-575-5000
Fax: 919-575-5023

FCI - Butner (Medium)
PO Box 1000
Butner, NC 27509
919-575-4541
Fax: 919-575-6341

FPC - Seymour Johnson (Closed 2006)
Caller Box 8004
Goldsboro, NC 27533-8004
919-735-9711
Fax: 919-735-0169

Oklahoma Federal Prisons

FCI - El Reno
PO Box 1000
Highway 66 West
El Reno, OK 73036-1000
405-262-4875
Fax: 405-262-6266

FTC - Oklahoma City
PO Box 898892
7500 MacArthur Boulevard
Oklahoma City, OK 73189-8802
405-682-4075
Fax: 405-680-4041

Ohio Federal Prisons

FCI/FPC - Elkton
8730 Scroggs Road
PO Box 89
Elkton, OH 44415
330-424-7448
Fax: 330-424-4539

Oregon Federal Prisons

FCI/FPC - Sheridan
PO Box 8000
27072 Ballston Road
Sheridan, OR 97378-9601
503-843-4442
Fax: 503-843-3408

Pennsylvania Federal Prisons

FCI/FPC - McKean
PO Box 5000
Bradford, PA 16701
814-362-8900
Fax: 814-362-3287

USP - Lewisburg
RD #5
Lewisburg, PA 17837
717-523-1251
Fax: 717-524-5805

FCI - Loretto
PO Box 1000
Loretto, PA 15940
814-472-4140
Fax: 814-472-6046

FCI - Schuylkill
PO Box 700
Minersville, PA 17954
717-544-7100
Fax: 717-544-7225

FPC - Allenwood
PO Box 1000
Montgomery, PA 17752
717-547-1641
Fax: 717-547-1504

FCI - Allenwood (Low)
PO Box 1500
White Deer, PA 17887
717-547-1990
Fax: 717-547-1740

FCI - Allenwood (Medium)
PO Box 2500
White Deer, PA 17887
717-547-7950
Fax: 717-547-7751

USP - Allenwood
PO Box 3500
White Deer, PA 17887
717-547-0963
Fax: 717-547-6124

South Carolina Federal Prisons

FCI - Edgefield
501 Gary Hill Road
PO Box 723
Edgefield, SC 29824
803-637-1500
Fax: 803-637-9840

FCI - Estill
100 Prison Road
Estill, SC 29918
803-625-4607
Fax: 803-625-3139

South Dakota Federal Prisons

FPC - Yankton
Box 680
Yankton, SD 57078
605-665-3262

Tennessee Federal Prisons

FCI - Memphis
1101 John A. Denie Road
Memphis, TN 38134-7690
901-372-2269
Fax: 901-382-2462

Texas Federal Prisons

FCI - Bastrop
Box 730
Highway 95
Bastrop, TX 78602
512-321-3903
Fax: 512-304-0117

FCI - Beaumont (Low)
PO Box 26025
Beaumont, TX 77720
409-727-8172
Fax: 409-626-3500

FCI - Beaumont (Medium)
PO Box 26045
Beaumont, TX 77720-6045
409-727-0101
Fax: 409-720-5000

USP - Beaumont
PO Box 26035
Beaumont, TX 77720
409-727-8188
Fax: 409-626-3700

FCI - Big Spring
1900 Simler Avenue
Big Spring, TX 79720-7799
915-263-6699
Fax: 915-268-6860

FPC - Bryan
PO Box 2197
1100 Ursuline
Bryan, TX 77805-2197
409-823-1879
Fax: 409-775-5681

FMC - Carswell
PO Box 27066
"J" Street, Building 3000
Fort Worth, TX 76127
817-782-4000
Fax: 817-782-4875

FPC - El Paso
PO Box 16300
SSG Sims Road, Bldg. 11636
El Paso, TX 79906-0300
915-566-1271
Fax: 915-540-6165

FMC - Fort Worth
3150 Horton Road
Fort Worth, TX 76119-5996
817-534-8400
Fax: 817-413-3350

FDC - Houston
1200 Texas Ave.
Houston, TX 77002-3505
713-221-5400
Fax: 713-229-4200

FCI - Seagoville
2113 North Highway 175
Seagoville, TX 75159
972-287-2911
Fax: 972-287-5466

FCI - Texarkana
PO Box 9500
Texarkana, TX 75505
903-838-4587
Fax: 903-223-4424

FCI - Three Rivers
PO Box 4000
Three Rivers, TX 78071
361-786-3576
Fax: 512-786-4909

Virginia Federal Prisons

FCI - Petersburg
PO Box 1000
Petersburg, VA 23804-1000
804-733-7881
Fax: 804-733-7881

Washington Federal Prisons

FDC - SeaTac
PO Box 13901
Seattle, WA 98198
206-870-5700
Fax: 206-870-5717

West Virginia Federal Prisons

FPC - Alderson
Glen Ray Road, Box B
Alderson, WV 24910
304-445-2901
Fax: 304-445-2675

FCI - Beckley
PO Box 1280
Beaver, WV 25813
304-252-9758
Fax: 304-256-4955

FCI - Morgantown
Greenbag Road
PO Box 1000
Morgantown, WV 26507-1000
304-296-4416
Fax: 304-284-3613

Wisconsin Federal Prisons

FCI - Oxford
Box 500
Oxford, WI 53952-0500
608-584-5511
Fax: 608-584-6371

Puerto Rico Federal Prisons

MDC - Guaynabo
P.O. Box 2146
San Juan, PR 00922
809-749-4480
Fax: 809-749-4363

Bring a Family Member

These are items that should be allowed, but don't be disappointed if they are not. Bring them with you and if they aren't allowed you will be given the opportunity to give them to a family member, have the items mailed back home, or donated to a local charity organization. If a family member is dropping you off, have them wait around so they can get any of your property that is not allowed. Keep in mind that it could take a few hours to be processed in, so let your family members know in advance. The personal clothes that you are wearing when you self-surrender will also be taken from you. You will be given some type of prison garb ("New Fish" clothing) to wear until you get issued your institutional uniforms. Your personal clothing items will be given the same three options as above.

Wedding Bands

A plain wedding band, if married, should be allowed as long as there are no stones attached to it, no exceptions. Eyeglasses, if required and their case will be allowed. False teeth will be given a thorough inspection but should also be allowed. No hairpieces! Some institutions will allow you to keep your t-shirt, underwear and socks that you wore in as long as they are white in color boxers or briefs, and no designer brands or styles.

Here is a little tip for you, wear boxers. Briefs are considered to be panties in male prisons.

A simple address book or plain piece of paper with addresses written on it will also probably be allowed.

Some institutions will allow a simple cross or other religious necklace to be worn but this is another one that you will want to call ahead on.

Medicines

If you are on any medicines that have been prescribed by a doctor, you definitely need to call ahead. The CO will confiscate prescription medicines and the institution's medical department in their place will issue new medicines. This is assuming that you have the proper legal prescriptions from your doctor for the medicines with you and only after the institution's medical staff has determined that you actually need them. Ask about the timeline on getting new medicines, once your medicines have been confiscated. You don't want to be between needed doses and have to wait a few hours or even days before you visit the medical department to get new prescriptions. Any type of walking cane or other medical equipment will also probably be confiscated and reissued by the prison's medical department. Remember to call ahead to be 100% sure about any medicines or medical questions that you might have. No over-the-counter medications of any type will be allowed.

Money

Money, my advice to you is to bring at least $250 to $500 in cash, or as much as possible, with you. It may take 3-6 weeks before you are assigned a job and another 4 weeks after that to get paid. That is a long time to go without being able to buy stamps or anything else you may want or need. Inmates in prison are provided with the basics. Inmates get fed, clothed, and given a dry place to sleep. There are no luxuries provided by the BOP or any state prison system. In prison a tube of toothpaste is considered a luxury that you will have to buy yourself. You will be issued a welcome kit which contains such items as a comb (no shampoo), a motel size bar of soap (no deodorant), a cheap plastic razor (no shaving cream), a thumb sized toothbrush, and if you are lucky, a bag of powder toothpaste which looks like bacon soda. The bar of soap is also used for deodorant, shampoo and shaving cream. These items are fine for a few days but you will want to buy better supplies from the institution's commissary as soon as you are allowed to shop. The money you bring with you will be placed into your Inmate Account. The Receiving CO will count the money in front of you and issue you a receipt. Read the chapter on the commissary to learn more about what shopping in prison is like.

If you have photographs of your family that you wish to take inside with you, I would bring them and see if they are allowed. In most cases, I believe, you will be told to have someone mail them to you.

Legal Papers

Legal papers and documents is another issue you will want to call ahead about. There is no sense in dragging 100 lbs. of paperwork in with you if it's not allowed. You are legally entitled to have paperwork pertaining to your case, but it will have to be approved.

Like I said, you can bring very little.

You're Living Space

You're House

You're house. The small 10'x 8' or 8'x 6' room that you get assigned to when you arrive at prison will be known as you're house. You're house, depending on the security level of the prison, will either be a cell or a cube. A cell will have the closing metal or iron bar door and, if you are lucky, a barred window that you may or may not be able to open slightly. Most prisons (not all) have no central air system so a slightly opened window is a blessing. A cube may also have a window, but will have no door. Cells are closed rooms with walls that connect to the roof. A cube is located in a large open room or unit that has walls approx. 5 ½ feet tall that you can look over. The inmate lying on the top bunk of cube #1 can see the inmate lying on the top bunk of cube #40. Just imagine a large office with individual workstation cubes and you will get the picture.

Your house will be located in a large building called a block or a unit. These can be several stories high or just a single level. If you are serving time at a low security prison your building's doors will be locked at all times, except during the 10-minute moves. If you are at a camp your unit's doors will remain unlocked 99% of the time. Remember, the lower security level of the prison, the more freedom you will have.

You will most likely share your house with at least one other inmate and possibly more. The house will be your responsibility to keep clean and a Safety CO will inspect it daily or weekly. Most cellys will share the duties of the cleaning, but some inmates will pay another inmate to keep their house clean. Your new celly should let you know if he has an arrangement with another inmate to clean the house. You may be asked to share the cost of the cleaning, which usually is around $2.00 a week. If you can't afford the $1.00 a week (your share) you will probably have to do all of the cleaning every other week. At some joints the Safety CO will pick the cleanest house and those inmates will be allowed to go to chow first for the next week. That is a big incentive to some inmates. Once you stand in the chow line for 30 to 45 minutes to eat you will understand better.

Your house is where you will spend the majority of your time while you are incarcerated. In the evening the majority of inmates will either be watching TV in the TV Room, or in their house reading a book.

Bunk Beds

Your house will usually have one or two bunk beds, lockers and a desk. The bunk beds may be the common type with the wavy type springs for support or just the metal plate type that is similar to lying on the floor. You may have a real mattress or just a vinyl-covered piece of foam. You may have a real pillow, or again, just a vinyl covered smaller piece of foam. When you first try sleeping on your new bed you will think that there is no way that your back will ever adjust to this bed. It will. The human body can, and will adjust to anything; inmates are living proof of that.

Unit Regulations

The following is taken from an Inmate's Admission and Orientation Handbook that is given to all new inmates when they arrive at prison or camp. This particular handbook was given out at the Federal Prison Camp located in Ashland, Kentucky. While some of these rules and regulations will differ slightly from prison/camp to prison/camp it should give you a good idea of what to expect.

Unit Regulations

With the exception of shoes, no items will be stored on the floor beneath the beds. Furthermore nothing can be stored beneath your mattress or pillow.

All cells or cubicles will be ready for inspection at 7:30 a.m. Beds will be made up in a uniform manner by 7:30 a.m., 5 days a week, regardless of job assignment. Inmates going on furlough, day pass, visiting room, etc. will have beds made and cells or cubicles clean prior to leaving. On weekends and holidays, all beds will be made once the inmate is out of bed. Failure to comply will result in disciplinary actions.

Each individual is responsible for maintaining his cell or cubicle in a neat and sanitary manner at all times.

Daily sanitation inspections are conducted. Plastic trash bags are not to be used in the cells or cubes for any reason. If an inmate's cell or cubicle is found dirty or untidy, he will be advised of same and disciplinary action may be taken.

No items will be attached to the unit, cell or cubicle walls.

No nude pictures will be displayed in the unit, cell or cubicles.

No wood or glass will be stored in the unit, cells or cubicles. Glass will not be permitted on the cell or cubicle desktops.

No contraband mirrors will be authorized in the cells or cubicles.

No items will be stored or placed on top of the cell or cubicle locker except a picture frame and a Bible. All other personal property will be stored inside the locker.

No excess clothing or shoes are allowed.

No smoking

No flammable items will be stored in the units. (Paints, lacquer, thinner, etc.)

Dirty clothing, towels, and linen will be deposited in the receptacles provided in the Clothing Room or laundry bags.

Television Viewing: The selection of programs to be viewed will be determined by the Unit TV Committee and approved by the Unit Manager. Special programs and sporting events will be viewed on the designated TV's. The initial program will be viewed in its entirety. Further TV regulations will be posted on the bulletin board in each unit. The TV Room will close at 11:30 p.m., Sunday through Thursday. Friday, Saturday and Holidays the TV Room will close at 3:00 a.m. The TV Room will open at 6:00 a.m.

Card Games/ Recreation Activities: All games and related activities will be conducted in the rooms provided in each unit. All game and card playing will be discontinued at 9:30 p.m. each evening in the main unit and at 10:30 p.m. in the utility room.

On weekend and holidays, quiet hours are in effect until 10:00 a.m.

Inmate Personal Property: Program Statement 5580.06, entitled "Personal Property, Inmate" defines personal property that each individual is authorized to retain. Additionally, please refer to the Institution Supplement No. 5580.06B, Standards of Attire, Personal Property, and Housekeeping Regulations. Both of these publications can be viewed in the Inmate Law Library. It is the responsibility of each inmate to become aware of this policy and adhere to the guidelines.

Each Bureau of Prisons facility will identify in local guidelines and procedures the type and amount of storage available for inmate's personal property in the facility's living unit. The guidelines will set specific limits, taking into consideration the number of inmates assigned to the living area. The amount of personal property allowed by each inmate will be limited to those items that can be neatly and safely placed/stored in the locker or space designated. Under no circumstances will any materials referred to in this policy be accumulated to the point where they become a fire, sanitation, security, or housekeeping hazard.

The amount of clothing allowed (civilian or institution) will be limited to those items that can be neatly stored in the space provided. Local guidelines may set specific item number limits, but such limits will not exceed the capacity of the specified area or locker designed for clothing.

Black or dark blue clothing is not authorized.

The following Institution Clothing is authorized per individual:

3 Pair Work Pants
3 Work Shirts
4 Undershirts
4 Undershorts
4 Pair Socks
1 Pair Safety Shoes
1 Belt
1 Jacket or Coat
3 Towels
2 Washcloths
1 Pillow
1 Pillow Case
2 Sheets
2 Blankets (1 in summer)
1 Laundry Bag

Any inmate who goes to court WRIT will pack his property and take it to R&D for storage. This means all PERSONAL property. All issued institution clothing should be returned to the laundry.

Inmate Civilian Clothing: No civilian clothing is allowed.

No institution white (Food Service Department, and/or Clinic Uniforms) will be authorized for wear during leisure time activities.

All inmates must be in their respective cells or cubes by 4:00 p.m. and 10:00 p.m., 7 days a week for the count.

There will be no showering after 9:55 p.m. or before 6:00 a.m. Showers will be closed during the workday for cleaning.

No visiting between cells or cubicles after 10:00 p.m.

Inmates will not visit in units other than the one in which they live.

Unit lights will be turned off at 10:30 p.m. No excessive or loud talking will be permitted. There will be no visiting between cells or cubicles, no talking in the sleeping area after lights out, no loud noises or disturbances in hallways, dayrooms, washrooms, or TV room. All lights including desk lights and reading lights will be turned off at 11:30 p.m.

Radio playing will be allowed with the use of earphones or ear buds only.

No bed changes will be made without the approval of the Unit Correctional Counselor.

Inmates will not move furniture from room to room. All rooms will be arranged in the same manner (placements of beds, lockers, etc.).

Horse playing will not be tolerated.

Inmates will not sit in one chair and put their feet in another chair.

The Unit Orderlies are responsible for the general cleaning of the units. However, it is the responsibility of each individual to assist in maintaining sanitation in the unit. In addition, each individual is responsible for his own area on a daily basis.

Unit Restrictions: Confined to the unit during non-working hours, with the following exceptions: meals, religious services, visiting, call-outs, team meetings, commissary privileges, and medical sick call. There will be no visiting between units.

Inmates must check the Call-Out sheet daily for any changes to his schedule or status.

Town Hall meetings will be held monthly.

The Unit Manager reserves the right to move any inmate for management reasons.

The back doors are for emergency use only. Inmates are not allowed to exit the back doors for any reason other than an emergency.

Inmates will not use garbage cans to sit on.

Bulletin Board

A permanent bulletin board is located in each housing unit wing. You are expected to review this bulletin board daily for pertinent information that might concern you. At no time should anything be removed from the bulletin board without prior approval from a staff member.

Read the Call-Outs Daily

Unit Management

Unit Management is designed to enhance the quality and delivery of correctional programs and services to inmates. Because the unit deals with a smaller number of inmates, it is better able to tailor its program to their needs, while increasing personal contact between the staff and inmates. The programs developed and administered are designed to fulfill the objectives of the Bureau of Prisons, which are secure confinement, appropriate punishment, deterrence, and rehabilitation.

Unit Objectives Are:

1. To divide large numbers of inmates into well-defined groups whose members are encouraged to identify with each other and with the Unit Staff. This develops a feeling that members of the unit share common goals and responsibilities.

2. To increase the frequency of contact and the quality of relationship between staff and inmates, by placing decision-making personnel in close proximity to the inmates.

3. To provide better observation of inmates, thereby enabling early detection of problems before they become too serious.

4. To regulate inmate behavior in such a way that they are held accountable for their actions and encouraged to exercise self-control.

5. To provide programs for each inmate which meets his needs, capabilities, and ambitions.

6. To place special emphasis on each of the following:

    - Adjustment
    - Acquisition and performance of work skills
    - Interpersonal communications
    - Positive self-esteem
    - Self-Motivation
    - Problem solving techniques
    - Realistic goal setting
    - Education/Training
    - Acquisition of other “life” skills (for example, literacy, reasoning ability, social education)

Each individual will conduct himself in an adult manner and not bring discredit upon the Correctional Institution.

Unauthorized contact with civilian personnel is strictly prohibited.

Case Manager

Case Managers are assigned to assure proper placement in the system. They assess your needs and those of the institution for program assignments. In addition, they also deal with Parole, Transfer, Furloughs, and Releases. They are an integral and essential segment of the Classification Team. Their hours are staggered in an effort to provide adequate coverage and to be available during non-working hours.

Upon assignment to a particular unit, a Case Manager and Correctional Counselor will be assigned to each inmate. The Case Manager and Correctional Counselor will be available in each unit.

Bureau of Prison's Program Statements, Institution Supplements, and memorandums will be available in the Law Library for your use.

Correctional Counselor

The Correctional Counselor has the responsibility of assisting you with your day-to-day problems including: job assignments, visiting list, inmate account information, quarters and bed changes, furloughs, etc. The Correctional Counselor is your initial contact and your representative on the classification team. In most cases, the Correctional Counselor can resolve your problems, including emergencies. If not, you will be referred to the appropriate Staff Member.

Open House – Classification

The Unit Team operates under an "open door" policy. You may request to see members of your Unit Team as needed. However, please use courtesy if you cannot be seen at the time of your request, and a Team Member will advise you when you may be seen. The Unit Management Complex will be closed each Wednesday from 12:00 p.m. to 4:00 p.m. to allow the Case Managers and Counselors to process paperwork.

The Classification Team meets every Wednesday starting at 1:00 p.m. in the Administration Building. Watch the call out sheet for your name. You should Report to the Visiting Room to await your time to appear before the Unit Team for Classification.

Inmate System Management

The Inmate System Management Department is responsible for carrying out the duties related to the Records Office, the Mail Room, and Receiving and Discharge (R&D). If you have questions concerning your Sentence Computation, Property or Mail, you may come to the ISM Department's Open House between the hours of 10:30 a.m. to 11:30 a.m., Monday through Friday.

Records Office

The Records Office is responsible for commitment documentation, computation of sentence, determination of release date, and method of release.

- Jail Time: Jail credit is controlled by Title 18 USC 3568 which states "The Attorney General shall give any such person credit toward service of his sentence for any days spent in custody in connection with the offense or act for which sentence was imposed". The U.S. Marshall having custody at that particular time must certify jail time.
- Good Conduct Time: Title 18 USC 3624(B) controls good Conduct Time. Good Conduct Time is the amount of time that may be credited toward the service of a sentence on a term of imprisonment of more than one year, other than a term of life. Good conduct time is based on the time in custody that the inmate actually serves. Good Conduct Time is automatically credited at the time that the Sentence Computation is prepared. The "Project Satisfaction Date", at the bottom of the Sentence Computation sheet, is the Projected Release Date giving credit for all Good Conduct Time which could be credit based on the time to be actually served on the sentence.

Parole

Inmates sentenced under the Comprehensive Crime Control Act of 1984 (CCCA) are not eligible for Parole consideration. If you were sentenced prior to the Crime Control Act of 1984 or are considered having a parolable case, contact your Case Manager

The Record Officc is rcsponsible for documenting the receipt of a Detainer and assisting you in connection with procedures under the Interstate Agreement of Detainer. When a Detainer is received, you and the Warden will jointly sign the notice of untried indictment, information, or complaint and the right to request disposition. Procedures under the Interstate Agreement of Detainer, apply to untried indictments, information, or complaints. State Parole

Violators or Probation Violators are not covered under these provisions.

You're Celly

You're Celly or Bunky

The person you will be spending the most time with in prison will be you're celly, or sometimes called your bunky. This is the person or persons you will be sharing a cell or cube with.

Your celly in prison is like a roommate at college. You should be able to trust each other (to a point) with almost anything. Your celly should be the person who gives you the most advice when you first arrive. He should be your guide and teacher. He should watch your back and warn you if something is going down just as you should watch his back. Your celly should listen to all of your problems and stories as you should listen to his. He should introduce you around to some of the inmates who live around your house. He should show you the proper way to make up your bed. When you first arrive your new celly should offer you certain items like toothpaste, soap, shampoo, or deodorant, if he has extra. Cellys should hold the other's mattress and pillow down if one of them goes to the Hole. When cooking a meal in the unit, cellys should always ask each other if he wants a portion. Most importantly he should answer all of your questions.

Usually cellys will do this for their new celly without asking them to. Believe it or not the majority of inmates in the lower security prisons and camps are decent people. Almost all of them will help another inmate, up to a point, if they can. They will do this because most of them remember what it was like for them when they first arrived at prison. Of course the higher up the security level of the institution you go to, you will find less and less of this type of goodwill.

Most cellys become good friends but that is not a sure thing. I have seen cellys who hated each other and have gotten into fights. Just like in a bad marriage, the longer you are around someone the more you find out about him or her to dislike. If you find that you can't get along with your celly you can request a transfer to another open cell or cube. The trouble with that is you could end up anywhere and with a celly that is worse than the one you left.

My advice to you is to give your new celly some time to warm up to you. Inmates hear a lot of stories about the BOP sending in undercover officers to prisons to gather information about certain things that are going on. Some inmates will not trust new inmates until they are sure that they are not hot (undercover officer). Be yourself and never try to force a friendship. It takes some time but you will gradually be accepted.

Schedule

Daily Schedule

Everything you do in prison or prison camp will revolve around the institution's schedule. From the time that you are awakened in the morning and until you are told to go to sleep that evening, will all be according to the schedule.

A Schedule

The following is an example of a camp's daily schedule. Most other institutions will have similar schedules:

Time	Monday - Friday
6:00 a.m.	Lights On
6:00 a.m. - 7:00 a.m.	Mainline (Breakfast)
6:15 a.m. - 7:30 a.m.	Linen & Clothing Turn-In (Tuesday & Friday)
6:45 a.m. - 6:50 a.m.	Pill Line
7:00 a.m. - 7:30 a.m.	Sign-Up For Sick Call
7:30 a.m.	Work Call
9:00 a.m. - 11:00 a.m.	Sick Call By Appointment (Mon - Tue - Wed - Fri)

11:00 a.m. - 12:00 noon	Mainline (Lunch)
10:45 a.m. - 11:30 a.m.	Linen & Clothing Pick-Up
10:45 a.m. - 11:45 a.m.	Commissary Open House (Tue)
11:45 a.m. - 12:00 noon	Pill Line
12:00 noon	Work Call
2:30 p.m. - 2:40 p.m.	Pill Line
4:00 p.m.	Count (Stand Up)
4:00 p.m. - 5:30 p.m.	Mainline (Dinner)
Or Immediately Following The Clearance Of The 4:00 p.m. Count	
4:30 p.m. - 6:00 p.m.	Commissary Sales (Tue)
6:00 p.m. - 6:30 p.m.	Special Purpose Sales
5:00 p.m. - 9:00 p.m.	Barber Shop (Mon - Fri)
9:15 p.m. - 9:20 p.m.	Pill Line
10:00 p.m.	Count / Lights Out

The evening meal will be called on a rotating basis according to the housing unit that achieved the highest weekly sanitation inspection score.

There will be certain expectations and announcements, which will be announced over the public address system throughout the day and evening hours.

Weekends & Holidays

Time	**Sat / Sun / & Holidays**
6:45 a.m. - 7:45 a.m.	Coffee Hour
7:30 a.m. - 7:45 a.m.	Pill Line
8:00 a.m. - 3:00 p.m.	Visiting Room Hours
10:00 a.m.	Count (Stand Up)
10:00 a.m. - 11:30 a.m.	Brunch
Or Immediately Following The Clearance Of The 10:00 a.m. Count	
12:00 p.m. - 12:05 p.m.	Pill Line
3:00 p.m. - 3:10 p.m.	Pill Line
4:00 p.m.	Count (Stand Up)
4:00 p.m. - 5:30 p.m.	Mainline (Dinner)
Or Immediately Following The Clearance Of The 4:00 p.m. Count	
10:00 p.m.	Count / Lights Out

Night Time

What the Night Time Is Like

Nights in most prisons are surprisingly quiet. That is not to say that some prisons don't have night owls up late trying to entertain everyone with their singing, rapping or yelling, but they are usually in segregated housing units (the Hole). All prisons have a lights out time when the CO's will turn off the unit's lights and expect everyone to turn-in for the night. In most cases this is usually after the evening count. Some institutions will allow you to turn on your desk light (if you have one) to read or write, but there is usually a cutoff time for those lights too. Most prison commissaries carry battery powered reading lights that you can purchase to read with at night, but these also usually have a cutoff time. The CO's will enforce these cutoff times if you try to squeeze in one more chapter or letter past that time. In some camps the CO's don't care if you are up reading or writing all night, as long as you are quiet and not disturbing anyone else. Ask you're celly about your unit's lights out policy.

Don't get caught visiting in another inmates cell or cube after lights out. The CO's won't tolerate being out of your house at night, talking too loud, or making noise.

Snoring is a very common occurrence in prison just as it is anywhere else. If you are lucky and get a cellie that doesn't snore, consider it a blessing. But even if your cellie sleeps quietly you can bet your bottom dollar that there will be one inmate, or several, living somewhere around your house that snores as loud as a train wreck. Earplugs are an option that many inmates use. Earplugs can be obtained from other inmates who work in maintenance or landscaping. You may get lucky and get some for free but, just like most everything else, you probably will have to pay for them. Earplugs are considered contraband in the housing units but most CO's will overlook them. Ask your cellie if he has an extra pair or knows who might. If you can't obtain a pair of earplugs try using wet toilet tissue stuffed in your ears. Your first couple of nights inside you will think there is no way that you will ever get a good nights sleep with all of the snoring, but you will eventually get use to it.

Inmates' talking in their sleep and inmates yelling out because of a nightmare is also pretty common. If this happens to you don't worry about it. You may hear a few jokes about it the next day but nothing more.

Almost all first time inmates will have trouble sleeping for a few days after they arrive. If you are normal, your thoughts at night will be filled with regret about the actions you took to land yourself in prison. These thoughts, and others, will probably keep you awake for hours at night. After you adjust to being in prison these thoughts, while still being present, won't overwhelm you and you should fall asleep easier.

Sneak Thieves

You will hear stories of sneak thieves coming into cells or cubes at night and stealing things. Although I have no doubt that at some prisons it occasionally does happen, as long as you keep your locker locked, I wouldn't worry about it.

Thoughts of inmate violence and sexual assaults may also keep you awake at night, but unless you have beef with another inmate I wouldn't worry about that either. In most prisons 98% of the inmates go to sleep at lights out. Remember that in most mediums and penitentiaries the inmates are locked down in their cells at night. The low security level institutions lock the housing unit doors to the outside but leave the cell doors open. These units have a CO assigned to them and will know if an inmate is up walking around. And at most camps where (supposedly) non-violent inmates are housed they have no unit CO's, the unit doors are unlocked and the cubes have no doors. Most inmates love sleeping, so again, I wouldn't worry about anything happening to you at night.

Some inmates will sleep with their radio headphones or ear buds on listening to the radio with some type of sleeping mask on. Other inmates for a price can make these sleeping masks or you can buy a sewing kit at the commissary and make your own. Most are made from a sweat headband and a piece of cloth material. Picture a sleeping mask that can be purchased at the airport and you will have an idea of what they look like. Sleeping with an institution knit hat on pulled down over your eyes is also very common.

The CO's make counts during the night, and that means a flashlight shined on you to make sure you are in your bunk. If you are buried under your cover and the CO cannot see you, he will pull back your cover or tap your bunk until you awaken and you look to see what is going on. Most CO's will not shine the light directly at your face when you are asleep, but some will.

Cleaning

Cleaning Your Area

Cleaning your area in prison will be an everyday event for most inmates. This memo, which was passed out to every inmate, will give you a good indication of how clean you will be expected to keep you living area.

Cleaning

The following memo is to provide each inmate guidance for keeping their personal areas (cubes/cells) and common areas (TV area, utility room, card rooms, microwaves, restrooms, showers, laundry rooms) inspection ready.

On the day of inspection, any cube/cell found to have a discrepancy will be thoroughly shaken down for contraband (this includes inside lockers) and incident reports (shots) shall be written as warranted.

Cubes/Cells

1. **Do not leave trash in trashcan during the day.**
2. **Do not put items under pillow.**
3. **Do not leave the unit without properly making your bed.**
4. **Do not leave items on shelves cluttered.**
5. **Do not leave clothing/towels hanging from beds.**
6. **Do not leave clothing/towels on beds or in the floor.**
7. **Do not leave trash can dirty.**

Common Areas (All Unit Orderlies)

1. **Do clean restroom sinks, urinals, toilets/stalls, and floors**

using #20 cleaner.
2. Do disinfect shower walls and floors using #23 cleaner.
3. Do dust TV rooms, sweep and mop floors using #23 cleaner.
4. Do clean unit microwaves.
5. Do clean laundry rooms, utility rooms and all commonly used areas in the unit.

Note: It is everybody's responsibility to keep your unit clean.

Safety Staff and the Institutional Duty Officer conduct weekly housing unit inspections. Inspections are conducted to eliminate Fire, Safety and Sanitation concerns within the housing units.

Points will be deducted from the unit's weekly scores to establish a weekly meal rotation. Use the institutional supplement as a guide to help you prepare your cell/cube or room for the weekly inspection. All common areas within the units and areas around the outside of the housing units will be evaluated and scored.

The following information was taken from the Institutional Supplement 5580.06c (Standards of Attire, Property, and Housekeeping Regulations.)

A clothing rack and bookshelf are provided to accommodate the orderly placement of the inmate's clothing.

Lockers are not to be defaced by attaching anything to the outside (except a towel rack and towel).

No scarves or knit work will be placed on lockers or shelves.

One regulation photograph frame from the Commissary is the only thing permitted on top of the locker.

Inmates will only be permitted to retain those legal materials that are necessary for their active legal actions. All legal materials for active and ongoing cases will be stored in the inmate's locker. Additional space may be requested by writing to the Unit Manager.

Commissary items must be stored in the inmate's locker.

Only 3 newspapers (up to 14 days old from the date of publication)
Only 6 magazines (within 3 months of the date of publication)
Only 5 personal books

Sanitation:

Each inmate is responsible for his own bed area, including walls, ceilings, floors, windows, doors, and bars. Nothing can block a window. Nothing is to be thrown out of the windows.

All beds will be made each morning prior to the 7:30 a.m. work call. Inmates who work irregular hours must make their beds by 9:00 a.m. daily.

Additional reasons to lose points in the units:

- Storing items under the beds, mattresses, pillows or covers.
- Plastic bowls are to be stored inside the lockers (except one gallon jugs and ice chests).
- Commissary items hanging on book shelf or locker.
- Commissary on the floor or under the beds.
- Boxes, bags, clothing, blankets, anything under the beds.
- Not keeping toilets, showers or sinks clean.
- Floor not being swept and mopped daily.
- Trash can full and needing cleaning (Trash cans are for trash only).
- Paper being placed in the light fixtures.
- Personal items on the bookshelf or locker tops.
- Improperly made beds (not made, no blanket or folded down sheet).

- **Extra sheets, blankets, mattress, or pillow.**
- **Improperly labeled containers or containers with another product in them.**
- **Mops not hanging up to dry by the mop head.**
- **Dirty water in the mop buckets.**
- **Common area floors, walls and ceiling not clean.**
- **Showers not clean.**
- **Common restrooms not clean.**
- **Water fountains, microwaves, and ice machines, TV's, not clean.**
- **Smoke barrier doors not closed. Being propped open with objects.**
- **Tampering with fire equipment (tamper tag missing on extinguishers, clothing hanging from sprinkler pipes, items hanging on sprinkler heads).**
- **Items being stored under stairwells (trash carts, trash cans, buffers, strippers).**
- **Any items in the room, cell/cube that is a violation of established policy or contraband.**

Use this guide to help your unit rank first in the weekly meal rotation.

Fire, Safety, Sanitation is everybody's responsibility.

Inmate Jobs

Work Assignments

Prisons are basically little cities that require full time workers to maintain. They need workers to cook, clean, wash, and repair anything and everything to keep their little city running smoothly. The skill level of inmate workers in prison is as high as at most industrial plants out in the free world.

All medically able inmates shall work. No exceptions. Trust me when I say that you will want to work. The day will pass much faster when you are at your assigned job. Jobs at most institutions are assigned very much like they are assigned at union plants. The most senior inmate will usually have the best job. If you happen to get stuck with a job that you don't like you will be allowed to request a transfer to another job (depending if an open position exists) after a reasonable amount of time.

Almost all inmates are paid for a full forty-hour week regardless of how many hours of the week they actually worked. In fact, a lot of inmates work less than 4 hours a day and I have seen a few inmates who only worked 1 hour a day. I believe that most prison officials expect inmates to try to do as little as possible. Most of those officials aren't disappointed. But even with an inmate labor force, most all job assignments get done, and done well.

All jobs have a staff supervisor that you will report to. Most of these CO's treat their assigned inmate workers much like any supervisor at any plant in the free world treats their workers. Some will joke and kid around with the inmates and some won't. All of the CO's will expect you to be at your job on time. If they catch you loafing (too much) or doing something that you are not suppose to be doing, they will fire you. If you get fired from a position your counselor will place you in the worst job assignment that is open, which is usually in the kitchen or behind a push lawn mower.

You will be paid an hourly wage for your work, but don't expect to get rich. Most jobs, except for UNICOR, pay rates (at the time of this writing) from .12 cents an hour up to .35 cents an hour. That is barely enough to pay for the necessary items from the commissary that you need, like deodorant and toothpaste. If you have restitution or court ordered child support to pay it will be deducted from your wages.

Most inmates have weekends and holidays off. Inmates are also eligible for a paid vacation after a year's time.

If you are a master carpenter, plumber, or an electrician you can bet your bottom dollar that you will be assigned to the Maintenance Department. If you have skills in the kitchen you will be assigned to Food Services. If you are a lawyer or teacher you may end up working as a tutor in the Education Department. If you do not possess any skills other than having a strong back you will probably end up in landscaping. If your health prevents you from working the more strenuous jobs then you will probably end up wiping tables during meals in the cafeteria or rolling up the plastic eating utensils into the paper napkins. But I will tell you that it will take a medical excuse from the Institution's Doctor to get you out of working those more strenuous jobs.

Each job has its advantages and disadvantages. Inmates in Food Service get to eat early and are usually served more to eat than the other inmates. Food Service inmates are also in the position to steal food from the kitchen and either sell it to other inmates or eat it themselves. Food theft sales in camps are probably one of the highest money producing hustles that inmates take part in. Like everything else, the higher the security level of the institution the harder it is to get away with. Taking food from the cafeteria or kitchen is no exception. At lows and higher, the CO's will usually search you upon your leaving the cafeteria. You may get away with taking an apple back to your unit, but I wouldn't guarantee it. In camps they have fewer CO's so searches are less frequent. The amount and type of food stolen from the kitchen, available for inmates to purchase, is staggering. Inmates carry a lot of this food out the cafeteria doors in relatively small quantities, but I have also seen boxes of food items being carried out the rear kitchen door. You will have the opportunity to purchase everything from cheese slices, spices, and hamburger patties, to loaves of bread, fried chicken, fish, and even steaks. Most food items are sold for just a few stamps. A hamburger patty may go for 3 stamps and a steak could sell for as much as 10 stamps or more. These items go very quickly and on most weekends you will find inmates cooking some very delicious meals in their housing unit microwaves.

Here is a tip for you. If you choose to buy stolen kitchen food, only purchase what you can eat in one meal and eat it as soon as possible. Inmates who keep stolen food hidden in their cells or cubes and are caught could receive a shot, a trip to the Hole, or both.

Inmates who work in the Maintenance Department will do all types of mechanical and construction jobs. Everything from poring concrete to repairing plumbing leaks. The prison system gets a lot accomplished with their inmate labor force and at very cheap rates. This is a great place to learn mechanical and construction skills that you can use upon your release. A lot of maintenance inmates at camps also make extra money by making and hanging wooden shelves in other inmate's lockers. Maintenance inmates have access to the institution's tools and as long as the tool count is right at the end of the workday, the Maintenance CO doesn't seem to mind. If you get assigned to the Maintenance Department it shouldn't take you long to find out if this type of hustle is taking place at your joint.

Inmates that work in the institution's Auto Shop will get to work on the institution's fleet of vehicles. This is a very desirable position and openings will be scarce. If you have automotive repair experience I would let you counselor know when you first arrive.

Most of the institution's orderly jobs are janitorial positions for whatever department they are assigned to. If you were looking for a relatively easy job then I would recommend a Unit Orderly position. Most units have a few orderlies that work Monday – Friday during the daytime. They will start their cleaning at approximately 7:00 a.m. There will also be a weekend orderly that will clean Friday and Saturday nights. Unlike other inmates' jobs the orderlies job duties are broken down to where most orderlies only work approx. 45 minutes to 1 ½ hours a day. The duties include sweeping, mopping, dusting, painting and the cleaning and restocking of the restroom and showers. The weekend orderly will work longer hours because he will have to do all of the jobs by himself. However the weekend orderly has Monday – Friday off, which is very attractive to a lot of inmates.

Inmates who work in the Landscaping Department will mostly be cutting and trimming grass in the spring/summer, raking leaves in the fall, and shoveling snow and spreading ice salt in the winter. Some inmates love it and some hate it.

The Federal Prison Camp in Ashland, Kentucky has a National Forrest work detail that allows some inmates to leave the camp and work at Wayne National Forrest, under the supervision of the National Park Rangers. This is strenuous work but it is outside of the fence and out in the Forrest for 8 hours a day. Most Wayne National workers said working the detail was almost like being a free man. A very nice work assignment!

In the Federal Prison system the most desired job for inmates is working in the higher paying (for prison) UNICOR factory. Unfortunately it is also one of the rarest positions to get assigned to. Once you have filled out the application you have to wait until your name is at the top of the list to get assigned to UNICOR. Some inmates wait for years before their name gets to the top of the list. Chances are if you are serving 3 years or less, you will probably have no opportunity to work in UNICOR. However, you still should fill out an application as soon as possible after you arrive. You may get lucky (it could happen)!

The following is taken directly from a UNICOR Inmate Handbook. You should read this to better understand why this is such a sought-after position. The information on taking a paid vacation also applies to most every other non-UNICOR inmate work assignment.

UNICOR (Federal Prison Industries, Inc.)

The United States Congress for the purpose of providing federal inmates with opportunities to learn trades and acquire skills while incarcerated created Federal Prison Industries (FPI) in 1934. FPI operates under the trade name UNICOR.

FPI's primary goals are to manufacture high quality products in a safety-conscious environment while providing meaningful employment to inmates incarcerated in the federal prison system. FPI intentionally parallels private industry by design to give employees ample opportunity to acquire work habits and job skills which will enable them to be competitive in the job market upon release.

Inmates are not eligible for UNICOR placement prior to being formally classified by A&O staff and assigned to a Unit Team. Even then, UNICOR Employment Applications must be completed and submitted through Unit Team members.

Applications arriving at UNICOR are evaluated and applicants are placed into one of the following categories:

Category 1: Inmates with prior UNICOR experience during their current commitment who have no break in custody.

Category 2: Financial Responsibility Program (FRP) referrals as determined by the Unit Team.

Category 3: Inmates who have a high school diploma or G.E.D. that has been verified by the Educational Department.

Category 4: All Others.

Applicants are then placed on the hiring list based upon their category and the date their application arrived at the factory. Hiring is done on an as-needed basis according to category. The hiring list is periodically updated and copies are forwarded to Unit Teams for reference purposes.

All Inmates or detainees who are currently under an order of deportation, exclusion, or removal may not be assigned to UNICOR.

UNICOR has a day shift and when required, an evening shift. Day shift begins with institutional work call at 7:30 a.m. and concludes at 3:30 p.m. Evening shift hours, when required, will be determined based on factory requirement. Prior approval must be granted before an inmate can be assigned to the evening shift.

Normally, new hires assigned to production-related jobs are required to participate in a 30-day vocational woodworking program. This program is designed to provide a general knowledge of woodworking principals prior to assignment within the factory. Inmates participating in this program are paid standard UNICOR wages.

Inmates assigned to the factory are paid on an hourly basis. Current wages are:

(These may have changed as of this writing)

Grade	Hourly Rate
5	.23
4	.46
5	.69

6	.92
7	1.15

Pay is posted to inmate commissary accounts on the seventh workday of the following month. Pay slips indicating the amount earned are distributed when pay is posted.

Inmates receiving pay grade one who consistently make contributions above and beyond their normal duties are eligible for premium pay, which is an additional .20 per hour. Such achievements include demonstrating leadership abilities, training new hires, or contributing to production efficiency.

Inmates receive double time for hours worked beyond their normal work schedule. Double time is also applicable for hours worked on weekends or holidays.

Promotions:

Generally, new hires begin at pay grade five. The only exception being those who possess prior UNICOR experience as specified in paragraph four below.

Promotions to higher pay grades are dependent not only upon the availability of positions but also on the inmate's qualifications and performance. Each position is allotted a maximum pay grade. Promotions cannot be granted above the available pay grade.

Promotion to grade four can be done at the discretion of the inmate's immediate supervisor. However, there is a nincty-day waiting period between promotions thereafter.

Inmates with prior UNICOR experience during their current commitment who have no break in custody will start at pay grade four. This includes all inmates transferred administratively for non-disciplinary reasons. Such inmates will receive consideration for accelerated promotions back to their former grades once hired, depending upon work performance and vacancies. However, they must be recommended for accelerated pay by the Supervisor and obtain the appropriate Department Head and the Superintendent's approval.

Vacation Pay:

Inmate workers are granted vacation credits when their continued good work performance justifies such. During the first year full time employees earn hourly vacation credit each month equal to one-half of a standard workday. Thereafter, they earn hourly credit equal to one standard workday. Part-time workers, when utilized, receive half credit.

Paid vacations can be taken after one year to the extent of accumulated hours, or can be worked for pay. To do either you must first complete a Request for Vacation Form, which can be obtained from the inmate payroll clerk located in the UNICOR Business Office.

If you decide to take vacation time off you must schedule your vacation within sixty days before or after your anniversary date. Normally, a one-year period must elapse between vacations.

The completed vacation form must be submitted at least one week before your scheduled vacation date. If you elect to receive pay for your accumulated hours indicate this on the form. In both cases your immediate supervisor and the appropriate Department Head must then endorse the form.

The following is taken from an Inmate's Admission and Orientation Handbook that is given to all new inmates when they arrive at prison or camp. This particular handbook was given out at the Federal Prison Camp located in Ashland, Kentucky. While some of these rules and regulations will differ slightly from prison/camp to prison/camp it should give you a good idea of what to expect.

Work Assignments

Assignments are based on institutional needs and the type of work you may qualify for. Factors considered in making job assignments include physical condition, educational level, general intelligence, previous work experience, and general attitude. Some of the different types of work available are listed below:

Food Service:	Cooks, Bakers, Butchers, Salad Men, Orderlies, Dishwasher Operators, Clerk
Clinic:	Orderlies
Education: Orderlies	Clerks, Tutors, Librarians,
Clothing Room:	Sanitation Workers
Maintenance	Landscape Workers, Building Orderlies, Carpenters, Plumbers Electricians
Units	Orderlies
Administration Building	Orderlies
UNICOR	Clerks, Laborers (Warehouse)
Business Office	Clerks
Power Plant	Orderlies
Front Entrance	Orderlies
Machine Shop	Orderlies

Chapel	Orderlies
Recreation Department	Orderlies
Driver	Orderlies
Garden	Orderlies
Safety	Orderlies

Inmate Rights

Inmate Rights & Responsibilities

Here are the Inmate's Rights and Responsibilities as per the BOP Inmate's Handbook.

Rights:

You have the right to expect that as a human being you will be treated respectfully, impartially, and by all personnel.

Responsibilities:

You have the responsibility to treat others, both employees and inmates, in the same manner.

Rights:

You have the right to be informed of the rules, procedures, and schedules concerning the operation of the institution.

Responsibilities:

You have the responsibility to know and abide by them.

Rights:

You have the right to be informed of religious affiliation and voluntary religious worship.

Responsibilities:

You have the responsibility to recognize and respect the rights of others in this regard.

Rights:

You have the right to health care, which includes nutritious meals, proper bedding and clothing, and a laundry schedule for cleanliness of the same, an opportunity to shower regularly, proper ventilation for warmth and fresh air, a regular exercise period, toilet articles and medical and dental treatment.

Responsibilities:

It is your responsibility not to waste food, to follow the laundry and shower schedule, to maintain neat and clean living quarters, to keep your area free of contraband and to seek medical and dental care, as you may need it.

Rights:

You have the right to visit and correspond with family members and friends, and correspond with members of news media in keeping with Bureau rules and institutional guidelines.

Responsibilities:

It is your responsibility to conduct yourself properly during visits, not to accept or pass contraband, and not to violate the law or Bureau rules or institution guidelines through your correspondence.

Rights:

You have the right to unrestricted and confidential access to the courts correspondence (on matters such as the legality of your conviction, civil matters, pending criminal cases, and conditions of your imprisonment).

Responsibilities:

You have the responsibility to present, honestly and fairly, your petitions, questions, and problems to the court.

Rights:

You have the right to legal counsel from an attorney of your choice by interviews and correspondences.

Responsibilities:

It is your responsibility to use the service of an attorney honestly and fairly.

Rights:

You have the right to participate in the use of the law library reference materials to assist you in resolving legal problems. You also have the right to receive help when it is available through a legal assistance program.

Responsibilities:

It is your responsibility to use these resources in keeping with the procedures and schedule prescribed and to respect the rights of other inmates to the use of the materials and assistance.

Rights:

You have the right to a wide range of reading materials for educational purposes and for your own enjoyment. These materials may include magazines and newspapers sent from the community, with certain restrictions.

Responsibilities:

It is your responsibility to seek and utilize such materials for your personal benefit, without depriving others of their equal rights to the use of this material.

Rights:

You have the right to participate in Education, Vocational Training and employment as far as resources are available, and keeping with your interests, needs, and abilities.

Responsibilities:

You have the responsibility to take advantage of activities, which may help you live a successful and law-abiding life within the institution and in the community. You will be expected to abide by the regulations governing the use of such activities.

Rights:

You have the right to use your funds for commissary and other purchases, consistent with institution security and good order, for bank and/or savings accounts, and for assisting family.

Responsibilities:

You have the responsibility to meet your financial and legal obligations, including, but not limited to, court-imposed assessments, fines, and opening restitution. You also have the responsibility to make use of your funds in a manner consistent with your family needs and for other obligations that you may have.

Your Money

You and Your Money

Money, some people don't associate being in prison and having a need for money. They think you are in prison so you don't need money, because there is nothing to buy. They think that the government will keep you fed and clothed while you are in their custody, which they do. An inmate can survive on only what the BOP provides, but they only provide the very basics. They don't provide postage stamps for your mail. They don't pay for telephone calls. They don't provide shampoo, deodorant, or tennis shoes. They won't give you a birthday card to send to your child, when their birthday rolls around. In short, they won't provide any items that are sold in their Commissary. I assume that Congress and the American taxpayers object to an inmate living in "luxury" by using deodorant, so they refuse to pay for it. It's just the system, and it's not going to change anytime soon, so there is no need to stress over it.

The truth is that an inmate requires some money to purchase a few items he might need to make himself feel somewhat normal. Your time will pass much more enjoyably if you can purchase a few items each month from the Commissary. Inmates do receive an income each month from their job assignments, but they are paid only $.12 to $.35 an hour. This will be enough to cover the basics each month but if you want something extra you will need someone to send you some money in. For those of you with families or friends, who can help you financially; consider yourself to be very, very blessed. You should write them every week and tell them how much you love them for any financial assistance that they give you while you are incarcerated. Trust me when I say that even receiving just $20.00 a month from the outside will go along way to making your life in prison or camp more comfortable. Most inmates get no outside money sent in. This is why most of them have some type of hustle working inside.

When you first arrive to self-surrender, bring some cash with you. There are some items that you should buy, as soon as possible, that all inmates consider being a necessity. Shower shoes are a must. No one should have to shower in bare feet in prison (think about it). A full sized toothbrush, real toothpaste, and shampoo are also a nice "luxury" to have. Another "luxury" item that other inmates will appreciate you purchasing is deodorant.

Buying a set of sweats or thermals will make sleeping in the wintertime warmer. Prison is cold in the winter.

Federal Prisons provide a free TV for inmates to watch but they have to purchase a personal radio and batteries to listen to it. All TV's are muted with their sound broadcast over a weak radio transmitter that only can be picked up within approximately 30' of the TV. Picture the local drive-in with the movie's sound broadcast through your car's radio and you will know what I'm talking about. The radio and batteries will cost around $40.00 to purchase.

The following is taken from an Inmate's Admission and Orientation Handbook that is given to all new inmates when they arrive at prison or camp. This particular handbook was given out at the Federal Prison Camp located in Ashland, Kentucky. While some of these rules and regulations will differ slightly from prison/camp to prison/camp it should give you a good idea of what to expect.

You and Your Money

When you are committed to the camp all money in your possession will be credited to your commissary account that is maintained by the Commissary Officer. You may receive reasonable amounts of money through your correspondents, but please request that all funds be sent to the National Lock Box location at the following address:

FEDERAL BUREAU OF PRISONS
(INSERT INMATE NAME HERE)
(INSERT INMATE REGISTER NUMBER HERE)
POST OFFICE BOX 474701
DES MOINES, IOWA 50947-0001

The institution mailroom at the Federal Correctional Institution, Ashland, Kentucky will no longer accept funds received from outside the institution effective October 15, 2004. Any funds received after that date will be returned to the sender with specific directions on how to send the funds to the National Lock Box. Please notify all persons who send you funds that they must send all funds to the National Lock Box mailing address (above) and adhere to the following instructions:

Instruct them NOT to enclose personal checks, cash, letters, pictures, or any other items in the envelope. Enclose only the allowable negotiable instrument. The National Lock Box cannot forward any items enclosed with the negotiable instrument to the inmate. Items, personal in nature, must be mailed directly to the Bureau of Prisons' where the inmate is housed.

Instruct them that they must have the inmate's committed name (no nicknames) and register number printed on all money orders, U.S. Treasury, state and local government checks; any foreign negotiable instruments payable in U.S. currency; and envelopes.

Instruct them that their name and return address must appear in the upper left hand corner of the envelope to ensure that their funds can be returned to them in the event that they can not be posted to the inmate's account.

All funds received will be processed within 24 hours so

inmate families and friends may need to allow for additional mail time to Des Moines, Iowa. Funds received on Friday will be posted on Saturday. Inmates will be able to check their commissary account at the Automated Inquiry Machine (AIM) to verify receipt of funds and by utilizing the Inmate Telephone System (ITS).

Commissary

Commissary Shopping

The Commissary offers for sale a wide variety of candies, toiletries, and sundry items. NO PURCHASES CAN BE MADE WITHOUT YOUR PERSONAL ID CARD.

One of the happiest days around prison or camp is the day that the inmates get to shop at the commissary. If you have the funds available in your Inmate Account you are allowed to shop from a wide variety of goods. Shopping days will be one or two days a week and inmates will be allowed to shop only once during the week.

All inmates have a spending limit per month that they will not be allowed to exceed. The BOP (at the time of this writing) allows their inmates to spend up to $290.00 per month. During the Christmas holiday season the Warden may choose to increase this amount by $50.00 or $60.00. State inmates may get a higher or lower amount. Once you have reached your spending limit you will have to wait until the next month rolls around to shop again.

This is also the day that some inmates will attempt to get other inmates to purchase them something from the commissary, by promising them they will repay them next week with interest. Do as you will, but I can almost promise you that 99% of the time you will not be repaid.
This is also the time that some inmates will attempt to sell you stamps that they have won gambling. They will sell you 20 stamps (usually all singles, no books) for $5.00 to $6.00 worth of commissary items that they select. This is a good deal if you were going to purchase stamps at the commissary. It's not a good deal if you weren't. Having single stamps is a sure sign to the CO's that

someone has been gambling. You are only permitted to have a total of 3 books of stamps (60 singles) in your possession at anytime.

Inmates must have their Inmate ID Card with them when they are shopping at the Commissary. Inmates must also have a correctly filled out Commissary List Order Form when they place their order. These order forms are available in the Commissary, and sometimes can be found in the Library. Take a few extra blanks forms with you so that you can have a completed form filled out before you arrive at the Commissary. You don't want to hold up the line by filling out a form when it's your turn to turn your order in. The Commissary CO, and the other inmates, will let you hear it if this happens. Once your order form had been turned in you will not be allowed to change or add to your order. Any mistakes on your order form that you made will not be refunded, returned, or exchanged.

Take your empty inmate laundry bag with you to carry back the purchased items to your unit.

Expect very long lines at the Commissary. If it's during the winter season you should plan on dressing as warm as possible as you could be standing in line outside for up to 2 hours.

The following is taken from an Inmate's Admission and Orientation Handbook that is given to all new inmates when they arrive at prison or camp. This particular handbook was given out at the Federal Prison Camp located in Ashland, Kentucky. While some of these rules and regulations will differ slightly from prison/camp to prison/camp it should give you a good idea of what to expect.

Commissary
(Trust Fund Operations)

The Commissary offers for sale a wide variety of candies, toiletries,

and sundry items.
NO PURCHASES CAN BE MADE WITHOUT YOUR PERSONAL ID CARD.

You are permitted to purchase items not to exceed a monthly limitation of $290.00

All items purchased with the exception of postage stamps will account against your monthly allowance.

Stamps: You may purchase a maximum of 60 first class stamps each week during regular sales.

The Commissary is open on Wednesday and Thursday from 12:15 p.m. to 3:00 p.m. and 4:30 p.m. to 6:30 p.m. Each inmate is allowed to shop once each week.

Commissary blank order forms are available only at the Commissary. Please complete your order form before you get into the Commissary.

It should be noted that the Commissary is closed one week every three (3) months for inventory purposes.

The following is an example of some of the items that can be purchased at the Commissary. I don't know about you, but I was very surprised at the amount and variety of items that inmates were allowed to purchase. When you think about going to prison you just don't picture yourself standing in a commissary line to buy sun block and pints of ice cream.

Please keep in mind that the items offered, and their prices, will differ from institution to institution. Inmates pay no sales tax.

The first number is the price and the number listed after the item is the maximum amount that can be purchased at one time, if that item has a limit. The maximum amount listed here is also the maximum amount you are allowed to have in your locker. You are not allowed to stockpile commissary items. Some inmates will run their own store out of theirs and other inmate's lockers. They will sell items on credit at a premium price, usually one-for-two exchange. The buying inmate will be expected to pay their debt on their next payday. They will also usually accept stamps as payment. Running a store is against regulations and if you are caught it will cost you a trip to the Hole and commissary restrictions. All amounts in your possession over the maximum amount listed here could be confiscated as contraband. This will depend on the CO that shakes down your locker.

The brand "Keefe" is sold at most every federal institution. They package a wide variety of quality food products at discounted rates.

Beverages & Drink Mixes:

6.95	Tasters Choice	(2)
7.95	Tasters Choice Decaf	(2)
2.45	Keefe Regular Coffee	(2)
.75	Orange Juice (Can)	(24)
.80	V-8 Juice (Can)	(24)
.90	BNA/STW Juice	(24)
1.50	Hot Chocolate	(10)
1.85	Tang Drink Mix	
1.70	Instant Tea Mix	(4)
2.15	Peach Drink Mix	
2.65	Green Tea	
3.60	Sugar Free Kool Aid	
.85	Gatoraid	
1.30	Non-Dairy Creamer (Powder)	(2)
3.80	Instant Milk	
1.15	Sugar Cubes	
1.65	Sugar Twin	

Meats: (Combo of 12 Total)

1.25 Chili W/Beans
1.30 Vienna Sausage
1.85 Pepperoni Slices
3.35 Chicken
1.30 Tuna
1.30 Mackerel
1.35 Beef Pot Roast
1.05 Beef Jerky

Sweats (Limit of 2 Sets) Mark Your Size:

S/M/L/XL/2XL/3XL/4XL

18.85 Pants
15.50 Shirt
23.40 Pants: 5XL
20.15 Shirt: 5XL

Candies:

.50 Starburst Candy
1.40 Starlite S/Free Mint
.55 Fire Balls
.95 Tootsie Pops
1.70 Vanilla Pudding
.95 Jelly Beans

Chips: (Combo Of 7 Total)

1.45 Ranch Pringles
1.40 Lays Potato Chips
1.40 Cheetos
3.15 Doritos
2.40 BBQ Fritos
3.15 Tostitos
1.90 Pork Skins

Cookies: (Combo Of 7 Total)

.65 Vanilla Cookies
2.50 Soft Batch Cookies
1.40 Vanilla Wafers

Crackers:

2.40 Chex-Mix
3.10 TownHouse Crackers
2.15 Zesta Crackers
1.65 Cheese Bites
2.50 Mixed Nuts
1.90 Raisins
1.80 Peanut Butter Crackers

Misc. Snack Items:

.50 Buttered Popcorn
1.70 Jalapeno Peppers
.70 Hot Sauce
1.85 Picante Sauce
2.20 Keefe Peanut Butter
2.85 Goya Sazon
2.60 Honey
1.90 Grape Jelly
1.20 Sharp Cheese Spread
2.35 Jalapeno Cheese Squeeze
2.60 Macaroni & Cheese
4.50 Captain Crunch
2.00 Detour Protein Bars
.70 Honey Buns (12)
3.00 Granola Bars
3.30 Oatmeal Variety (Instant)
1.25 Peanut Butter Wafers
2.55 Soy Sauce

Shaving Accessories:

8.20	Shaving Bag	
7.30	Schick Twin Blades	(1)
8.10	Sensor Blades	(1)
1.75	Lather Shave	(1)
3.00	Magic Lotion	
1.75	Spice Shave Lotion	
10.10	Mach III Razor	(1)
3.50	Magic Shave Powder	
3.50	Magic Shave Smooth	
9.55	Mach III Blades	
3.00	Bump Stopper	
2.20	Magic Shave Gold	

Cosmetics & Deodorants:

1.40	Roll-On Deodorant	(2)
4.75	Vaseline Lotion	(1)
2.40	Degree Deodorant	(2)
3.50	Right Guard Deodorant	(2)
2.00	Baby Oil	(2)
2.00	Noxzema	
6.05	Clearasil Cream	
2.30	Next One Lotion	(2)
3.55	St. Ives Lotion	(2)
1.05	Petroleum Jelly	
3.60	Foot Powder	(1)
1.95	Bath & Shower Powder	
.85	Emery Boards	
1.10	Toenail Clippers	(1)
1.10	Tweezers	(1)
5.80	Mustache Scissors	(1)
.85	Small Nail Clippers	(1)
1.30	Cocoa Butter Strips	

Soaps: (3 Bar Limit)

1.85	Tide Detergent	(4)
.50	All Detergent	(5)
2.70	Bounce Softener	
.90	Dial Soap	
.90	Tone Soap	
2.20	Ambi Soap	
.80	Irish Spring Soap	
.60	Jergens Soap	
1.60	Dove Soap	
3.45	Neutragena Soap	

Shoes & Sporting Goods:

4.45	Shower Shoes S 7-8, Med 9-10, L 10-11, XL 12-14	(1)
1.95	White Socks	(2)
7.80	Mesh Bag (Laundry Type)	(1)
1.85	Black Kiwi Liquid	(1)
3.40	White Polish	(1)
3.65	Shoe Brush	
1.95	White Shoe Laces	
1.95	Black Shoe Laces	
2.60	Wrist Sweatband	(2)
1.95	Head Sweatband	(2)
5.20	Odor Eaters	(1)
3.60	Ball Cap	(1)
4.85	Orange Rain Poncho	
3.45	Mouth Piece	(1)
3.90	Tennis Balls	(3)
3.75	Racquet Balls	(2)
13.00	Waist Trimmer Up To 3XL	
7.80	Grey Shorts Up To 3XL	(2)
10.40	Grey Shorts 4X	(2)
3.90	Jock Straps Up To 3XL	(2)
9.10	X-Large Mesh Bag	(1)
1.05	Jersey Gloves	(1)

Hair Care Products:

4.25	Dark & Lovely Shampoo	
4.25	Dark & Lovely Conditioner	
7.80	Clipper Disinfectant	(1)
6.50	Pantene Shampoo/Conditioner	
1.85	Alberto VO5 Shampoo	(2)
1.60	Heritage Conditioner	(2)
5.75	Head & Shoulders	(2)
.95	Styling Brush	
2.80	VO5 Styling Gel	
2.60	Protein 29 Conditioner	(2)
5.55	Sulfur 8 Conditioner	(2)
3.00	Murray Soft-N-Sheen	(2)
2.75	Murray's Pomade	(2)
5.60	Pink Oil Moisturizer	(2)
.25	Comb 9"	(1)
.50	Afro Pick	(1)
.55	Super Comb	(1)
2.75	Club Brush	(1)
2.40	Wave Cap	(1)
2.85	Beeswax	(1)
.55	African Hair Rubber Bands	
6.25	African Pride Hair Grease	

Dental Hygiene: (Limit Of 2 Tubes Of Toothpaste)

1.55	Dental Floss	(1)
3.65	EfferGrip	(1)
2.40	Close Up	
2.20	Colgate Whitening	
2.75	Crest	
.95	Toothbrush	(1)
.45	Toothbrush Holder	(1)
1.55	Denture Cup	(1)
1.20	Denture Brush	(1)
3.45	Denture Toothpaste	(1)

1.30	Mouthwash	(1)

(Limit of 1 Tube)
6.00 Sensodyne
1.80 Ultra Bright

Thermal: (Limit Of 2 Sets)

4.90 Shirt: S,M,L,XL
5.85 Pants: S,M,L,XL
7.80 Pants Or Shirt: 2X, 3X

Watch Batteries:

2.35 #ECR 2016

Batteries: (Total Of 4 Packs)

2.20 Size AA (4 PK)
2.20 Size AAA (4 PK)

Miscellaneous Items:

.60	Writing Pen	(1)
1.70	Sewing Kit	(1)
2.25	Address Book	(1)
1.40	Chapstick	
4.50	Insect Repellant	(1)
(One Pair Of Sunglasses)		
6.50	Wrap Around Sunglasses	(1)
2.45	Aviator Style Sunglasses	(1)
3.90	Clip-On Sunglasses	(1)
1.05	Ponytail Holders	
11.05	Alarm Clock	(1)
11.45	Reading Light	(1)
3.65	Bulb For Light	
1.85	Drinking Mug	(1)
1.25	Bowl	(1)

4.69	Typing Ribbon	
2.99	Correction Ribbon	
2.55	Photo Album	(1)
.95	Q-Tips	
.75	Flyswatter	
2.20	Locker Mirror	(1)
.55	ID Card Protector	(1)
(Only 2 Decks Of Playing Cards)		
2.45	Playing Cards - Red Or Blue	
2.55	Pinochle Cards	
.95	Legal Pad	(2)
.15	Envelopes (10 x 15)	(6)
1.60	Utensil Set	
7.55	Koss Headphones	(1)
.75	Handkerchief	(5)
.65	Soap Bar Box	(1)
.25	Clothes Hanger	(5)
3.55	Sun Screen SPF 30	
4.60	Gold Watchband	(1)
6.25	Thermos Jug	(1)
6.40	Combination Lock	(1)
26.00	Weight Belt S,M,L,XL	(1)
9.10	Wrist Wrap	(1)
16.90	Atlas Weight Lifting Gloves	(1)
14.30	Knee & Elbow Wrap	(1)
5.40	Prayer Oil	(1)

T-Shirts: (Limit Of 2)

3.05	Tank Top S,M,L,XL
3.90	Tank Top 2X,3X
5.60	T-Shirts S,M,L,XL,2X,3X
7.80	T-Shirts 3X,4X
16.75	T-Shirts 5X
(Limit Of 7 Boxer Briefs)	
8.35	Boxer Briefs S,M,L,XL
11.20	Boxer Briefs 2XL

Greeting Cards:

5.10	Thinking Of You	(6)
5.10	Birthday	(6)

Non-Prescription Medicines:

1.75	Saline Nasal Spray	(1)
1.35	Aspirin	(1)
2.50	Ibuprofen	(1)
3.30	Liquid Antacid	(1)
2.25	Non-Aspirin	(1)
1.60	Antifungal Cream	(1)
1.50	Hydrocortisone Cream	(1)
3.55	Hemorrhoid Ointment	(1)
2.15	Milk Of Magnesia	(1)
1.95	Medicated Chest Rub	
2.15	Artificial Tears Drops	(1)
1.50	Allergy Tablets	(1)
3.45	Laxative Tablets	(1)
2.15	Tussin Cough	(1)
.70	Halls, Lemon	
.70	Halls, Cherry	
.80	Rolaids	
2.05	Tums (3 Pack)	
3.40	Vitamin E	
2.75	Multi-Vitamins	
2.15	Vitamin C	
2.55	Garlic Pills	
2.10	Muscle Balm	

Bag-A-Soup: (Limit Of 30)

.25	Chili Soup
.25	Chicken Soup
1.05	Long Grain White Rice
1.60	Refried Beans
.80	Tortillas

Sodas: (Limit Of 24 Cans)

1.90 Diet Coke 6-Pack
1.95 Classic Coke 6-Pack
1.90 Mellow Yellow 6-Pack
.35 Spring Water Single
1.90 Sprite 6-Pack

Kosher Meals: (Limit Of 14)

3.80 Chicken & Noodles
3.85 Beef Stew
3.20 Pasta W/Veggies
3.00 Vegetable Stew

Candies: (Combo Of 12)

.55 Hershey Candy Bar
.50 Snickers Bar
.50 Three Musketeers Bar
1.80 Crème Savers

Fruits: (Combo Of 20 Total)

Prices Are Seasonal
Bananas
Apples
Oranges
Peaches
3.35 Pitted Dates
.65 Lemon Juice

Ice Cream: (Limit Of 2 Pints Only)

.35 Orange Sherbet Bars (8)
1.65 Vanilla
1.65 Cookies & Cream

1.65	Cherry Vanilla		
.50	Drumsticks		(2)

Shoes: (Only 1 Pair)

31.20	Reebok Classic	SZ_______	(1)
65.00	Rockports	SZ_______	(1)
58.50	Asics Gel	SZ_______	(1)
54.60	Nike Low Post	SZ_______	(1)
80.60	Wolverine	SZ_______	(1)

Watches: (Limit Of 1)

31.60	Gold Timex
34.15	Silver Timex
33.30	IronMan Timex
8.45	Watchband, IronMan

Small Appliances:

11.60	Calculator	(1)
28.60	Norelco Trimmer	(1)
27.05	Beard Trimmer	(1)
36.90	Sony Radio	(1)
15.35	Electric Clip-On Fan	(1)

PRICES ARE SUBJECT TO CHANGE WITHOUT NOTICE!

Laundry

Clothing & Laundry Regulations

You have a choice of either dropping your dirty laundry off at the Institution's Laundry Room or using your unit's washers and dryers to clean and dry your own laundry. At most institutions you will have 2 days of the week (usually Tuesdays and Fridays) to drop your laundry off at the Laundry Room to be washed and dried. This will also be the time that you can exchange your dirty bedding sheets and blankets for clean ones. Like everywhere else, be prepared for long lines at the Laundry Room.

You are required to change your bedding linen each week. You will carry your dirty bed linen to the Institution's Laundry Room. When exchanging your bedding linen you must have the exact number of pieces that were issued to you. Exchanging only your sheets or blanket is not allowed. The CO will watch you drop each piece into the laundry hamper to verify that you are dropping off a complete set. You will be given a new bedroll that will contain:

2 Sheets

1 Pillow Case

1 Blanket (2 in winter)

From time to time the Laundry CO will do an inspection of each inmate's bed and locker to determine if they have more than the allowed amount of issued clothing and bedding items. If you get caught with more than what was issued, the CO will usually just confiscate the extra items without writing you a shot but this is not always the case. Depending on the CO, you could be written a shot.

After picking up you clean bed linen you are required to make your bed up as soon as you get back to your unit. When leaving your house to take your dirty bedding to be exchanged at the Laundry Room you should roll your mattress up. This will let the CO know that the reason your bed is not made up is because you are exchanging linen. I would also lock your pillow in your locker when you leave. They have a way of walking off.

Here is a tip. Many inmates prefer to wash their own bedding in their unit's washers and dryers because they are happy with the blanket they have. When you exchange bed linen at the Laundry Room you may receive a blanket that is a torn, stained, or not as warm as the one you dropped off. If you do receive a blanket that is not up to your standards don't try and exchange it again until the next laundry day. The Laundry Room CO won't want to hear that story.

Your dirty laundry (not your bed linen) must be placed in the institutional laundry bag that was issued to you when you arrived. These laundry bags are nothing more than nylon nets with a pull string to close the open end. Picture a lobster net and you will get the idea. Your laundry bag should have your name and inmate number written in permanent marker somewhere on it. When you take your laundry to the Laundry Room you must have the drawstring open end of the bag pulled tight and tied into a knot. It is not enough to have the string tied into a knot. You must also have part of the bag itself tied into a knot. This is to prevent your laundry bag from opening during a wash or dry cycle. The Laundry CO will place a large numbered safety pin onto your bag and write your name onto a logbook page next to the safety pin's number. This will match you up with the proper laundry bag when you come back to pick it up. You will be required to show your Inmate ID Card when picking up your laundry.

Your laundry bag along with others will be thrown into the large washers and dryers for cleaning and drying. Depending on the color of your institutional clothing you may get some bleed over from the colored items onto your whites. You also will have very wrinkled clothes when you take them out of the bag. These are the reasons why some inmates prefer to wash and dry their own laundry.

Most housing units will have a few washers & dryers for inmates to use. Laundry detergent and dryer fabric softener sheets are available for purchase at the Commissary. You will use your issued laundry bag to hold and carry your dirty clothes back and forth from your house to the unit's laundry room. Washing & drying other inmate's clothes is a hustle for some inmates and they make a nice amount of money doing it. If you plan on washing your own clothes then you will probably want to avoid doing so during the times that the inmates with the hustle is washing & drying. They get very upset when you are using the washer & dryer during their regularly schedule times. Some of these inmates have been washing & drying clothes at the same time of the day for years. If you do happen to wash your clothes during this time don't be surprised to find your wet laundry sitting on top of a dryer or on the floor. Other times you will see some inmates becoming upset because someone has taken their still damp laundry out of the dryer and placed it on top of that dryer. If your clothes have finished washing and the dryers have dry clothes in them you should ask around the unit to see whom they belong to. These inmates are usually watching TV and have forgotten about their clothes in the dryer. If you can't locate the owner of the clothes after asking around you will have to decide if you want to take them out and place them on top of the dryer or continue to wait. If the clothes are dry then "usually" you will be okay in placing them on top of the dryer. If you do decide to take the clothing out of the dryer try placing the clothing on top of the dryer as neatly as possible instead of in a big pile. This is called being courteous and respectful.

Just like at a coin laundry in your neighborhood back home, if your clothing is to be stolen from you it will happen while it is being dried. I would recommend staying close to the laundry room while you are washing and drying your clothes. Some inmates will take a book and read while their laundry is being washed and dried. This is the reason why you should have your name and inmate number written in large letters with a permanent marker on any non-uniform piece of clothing you may have. Commissary bought sweatshirts and sweat pants all look the same if they are not marked with some identifying name and number. If you don't have your name and number written on your clothing item, you will have only yourself to blame when it gets stolen.

The following is taken from an Inmate's Admission and Orientation Handbook that is given to all new inmates when they arrive at prison or camp. This particular handbook was given out at the Federal Prison Camp located in Ashland, Kentucky. While some of these rules and regulations will differ slightly from prison/camp to prison/camp it should give you a good idea of what to expect.

The Clothing Room is open for business on Tuesday and Friday only.

Laundry Hours: Turn-In: 6:15 a.m. – 7:30 a.m.

Pick-Up: 10:45 a.m. – 11:30 a.m.

Soiled clothing issue items will be dropped in the clothing containers located in the clothing room. Upon arrival, you will be issued the following:

3 Pair Work Pants	3 Towels
3 Work Shirts	2 Washcloths
4 Undershirts	1 Pillow
4 Undershorts	1 Pillow Case
4 Pair Socks	2 Sheets
1 Pair Safety Shoes	2 Blankets (1 in Summer)
1 Belt	1 Laundry Bag

1 Jacket or Coat

Clothing Room Personnel will make clothing repairs for government issued clothing. Repairs of civilian clothing, i.e., replacement of buttons and repair of small tears, may be accomplished by use of the unit sewing kit that is sold in the Commissary.

Blankets can be exchanged as available in the Clothing Room during sheet exchange.

The only issue clothing that you are authorized to have in your possession are those items that were issued by Clothing Officer.

Safety shoes will be issued to all inmates and must be worn on the job assignment.

Upon release from this facility, all issued clothing must be returned before clearance is given.

Dress Code

Work Dress Code

Only issued institution uniforms are to be worn during working hours. Steel-toed boots must be worn on all work details.

Shirts must be tucked into pants/trousers and belt must be buckled.

Pants/trousers will not be tucked or bloused into boots.

Issued institution clothing cannot be mixed with sweat pants/sweat shirts or athletic clothing. Issued institution clothing may not be worn with athletic shoes.

Food Service workers are not permitted to wear white Food Service clothing with issued institution clothing or personal/athletic clothing.

Shower shoes are not to be worn outside the living quarters.

Food Service Meal Time Dress Code

No hats/caps will be worn in the dining room at any times.

During Duty Hours (Monday - Friday): Inmates must wear their issued institution clothing or authorized work uniforms.

After Duty Hours (Including Saturday, Sunday and Holidays): Personal/Athletic clothing is permitted to be worn. (This does not apply to Food Service workers on duty).

Shirts must be tucked into pants/trousers/shorts.

Shoes and socks must be worn.

Clothing must be clean and unaltered.

No sleeveless shirts/t-shirts will be worn.

Pants will not be tucked/bloused in boots.

Meals

The Food Service Administrator and Food Service Staff are responsible for all aspects of the Institution's Food Service Program. In addition, they plan and supervise a training program in all areas of food service. Work assignments in food service provide an excellent opportunity to learn a food service or baking skill.

Prison meals taste bland, to say the least, but are sometimes surprisingly good. You will be served 3 meals a day in the institution's cafeteria. Inmates, under the direction of the Food Service CO, will prepare all meals. The amount of food that you will be served will remind you of a high school cafeteria. Like everything else in prison, you will usually have to wait in long lines to eat. Meals will be served on plastic trays with plastic utensils. Most Federal Institutions will have self-serve salad bars and fountain drinks. Don't expect Coke or Pepsi at the fountain machines. You will usually have a choice of lemonade, orange drink, iced tea (sweet or un-sweet), or water. Milk is usually only served at breakfast and brunch.

Kosher meals are available for some inmates because of their religious beliefs, but the Institution's Chaplin must approve this. Non-meat entrees will also be available upon request and when available. No special meals are prepared for vegetarians. If you are a vegetarian you will just have to eat from the salad bar and whatever else non-meat items you can find that is being served.

Institutional uniforms, with boots, must be worn to breakfast and lunch, Monday - Friday. Casual dress is usually okay for dinner and at all meals on the weekends and holidays. No hats or head wraps will be worn at anytime. No radio headphones will be worn at anytime.

The following is an example of a one-week menu from a Federal

Institution. The BOP usually has a 5-week rotating menu. This means you will see the same week's menu every 5 weeks.

During special holidays, Christmas & Thanksgiving, there will be special meals served. Once a year you might get served a real steak.

Prison leftovers, from previous meals, are made into a soup that is called "Soup De Jour". You will see a lot of it!

Menus are subject to be changed without notice.

Sunday:

Coffee Hour:

Coffee Cake or Fresh Fruit

Dry Cereal

2% or Skim Milk

Coffee

Sugar (6 pks max.)

Brunch:

Chilled Fruit Juice

Grilled Eggs or Boiled Eggs (2)

Cream Beef & Gravy

Soy Available

Home Fries or Boiled Potatoes

Biscuits

Margarine

Asst. Jelly (3 pks max.)

2% or Skim Milk

Coffee

Sugar (6 pks max.)

Dinner:

Soup De Jour

Chicken Fried Steak

Stroganoff Available

Chicken Gravy

Mashed or Boiled Potatoes

Broccoli Casserole

Tossed Salad

Asst. Dressings

1 Slice of Wheat Bread

Margarine

Chilled Peaches

Asst. Beverages

Monday

Breakfast:

Chilled Fruit Juice

Biscuit W/Gravy

Grits

Margarine

2% or Skim Milk

Coffee

Sugar (6 pks max.)

Lunch:

Chicken & Rice Soup

Over Fried Chicken or Baked Chicken

Oven Glo Potatoes

Pinto Beans

Salad Bar

1 Slice of Wheat Bread

Margarine

Ice Cream or Fresh Fruit

Asst. Beverages

Dinner:

Pepperoni or Cheese Pizza (2 Slices)

Asst. Snack Chips or Pretzels

Salad Bar

Fresh Fruit

Asst. Beverages

Tuesday

Breakfast:

Chilled Fruit Juice

Chocolate Eclairs

Dry Cereal

2% or Skim Milk

Coffee

Sugar (6 pks max.)

Lunch:

Egg Drop Soup

Egg Rolls

Chicken Fried Rice or Steamed Rice

Salad Bar

Chocolate Cake W/Icing or Fresh Fruit

Asst. Beverages

Dinner:

Soup De Jour

Grilled or Baked Hamburgers

Soy Patty Available

French Fries or Baked

Lettuce/Onions/Pickles

Mustard/Ketchup

Salad Bar

Chilled Fruit

Asst. Beverages

Wednesday

Breakfast:

Chilled Fruit Juice

Asst. Iced Donuts

Farina

2% or Skim Milk

Coffee

Sugar (6 pks max.)

Lunch:

Chicken Nuggets or Baked

Soy Ala King Available

Macaroni Salad or Mac & Tomatoes

Peas & Carrots

Salad Bar

1 Slice of White Bread

Margarine

Cherry Crisp or Fresh Fruit

Asst. Beverages

Dinner:

Breaded Pork Chops or Baked

Peanut Butter Sandwich Available

Baked Potato

Sour Cream

Steamed Corn

Salad Bar

Biscuits

Margarine

Fresh Fruit

Asst. Beverages

Thursday

Breakfast:

Chilled Fruit Juice

French Toast W/Maple Syrup (Diet Syrup Available)

Oatmeal

Margarine

2% or Skim Milk

Coffee

Sugar (6 pks max.)

Lunch:

Soup De Jour

Nachos

Soy W/Taco Seasoning Available

Cheese Sauce

Pinto Beans

Sour Cream

Salsa

Salad Bar

Pudding or Fresh Fruit

Asst. Beverages

Dinner:

Soup De Jour

Tuna Salad Sandwich or Plain Tuna

Cheese Sandwich Available

Misc. Snack Chips or Pretzels

Steamed Broccoli

Lettuce/Tomato/Onion

Salad Bar

Asst. Cookies or Fresh Fruit

Asst. Beverages

Friday

Breakfast:

Chilled Fruit Juice

Sweet Rolls

Dry Cereal

2% or Skim Milk

Coffee

Sugar (6 pks max.)

Lunch:

Soup De Jour

Meatball Sub

Soy Sloppy Joe Available

French Fries or Baked

Salad Bar

Chocolate Glazed Brownie or Fresh Fruit

Asst. Beverages

Dinner:

Baked Fish Fillet

Cottage Cheese

Macaroni & Cheese or Mac & Tomatoes

Steamed Carrots

Salad Bar

1 Slice of White Bread

Margarine

Chilled Fruit

Asst. Beverages

Saturday

Coffee Hour:

Sweet Rolls or Fresh Fruit

Dry Cereal

2% or Skim Milk

Coffee

Sugar (6 pks max.)

Brunch:

Chilled Fruit Juice

Grilled or Boiled Eggs (2)

Sausage Patty

Soy Patty Available

Biscuit W/Jelly

Country Gravy

Grits

Margarine

2% or Skim Milk

Coffee

Sugar (6 pks max.)

Dinner:

Cream of Broccoli Soup

Roast Turkey

Chicken Stew Available

Mixed Vegetables

Mashed or Boiled Potatoes

Gravy

Salad Bar

Dinner Rolls

Margarine

Fresh Fruit

Asst. Beverages

Mail

Inmate Mail

Mail Call will usually be after the evening meal, Monday – Friday (except holidays). Mail at lows will be distributed in the housing units. Mail at camps will usually be distributed at a central location. Each camp housing unit will be called one at a time to get their mail. Some CO's will allow other inmates to pick up mail for other inmates, some won't. The inmate it is addressed to must pick up all legal mail.

The Mail Room processes all incoming/outgoing mail Monday through Friday. Mail is not processed on weekends or holidays.

Two mail depositories are usually located just outside the entrances to the Unit Management Complexes. One of these depositories is marked "Special Mail". Only mail that meets the criteria for "Special/Legal Mail" is to be placed in the depository marked "Special Mail". All other mail is to be placed in the depository marked "General Mail".

Mail will be collected from the depositories at 6:30 a.m., Monday through Friday, excluding holidays.

All incoming mail general correspondence and approved packages will be opened and checked for contraband by Staff. Incoming mail that meets the criteria established for "Legal Mail" will only be opened in the presence of the inmate.

Special Mail from Attorneys:

To the inmate: It is suggested you provide the following information for special mail privileges to your attorney(s), at the earliest opportunity.

To the attorney: The Bureau of Prisons Program Statement on correspondence provides the opportunity for an Attorney who is representing an inmate to request that Attorney-Client correspondence be opened only in the presence of the inmate. For this to occur, Bureau Policy requires that you adequately identify yourself as an Attorney on the envelope and that the envelope be marked "Special Mail - Open Only In The Presence Of The Inmate" or with similar language. Provided the correspondence has this marking, Bureau Staff will open the mail only in the inmate's presence for inspection for physical contraband and the qualification of any enclosure as "Special Mail". The correspondence will not be read or copied if these procedures are followed. If your correspondence does not contain the required identification that you are an Attorney, a statement that your correspondence qualifies as "Special Mail", and a request that the correspondence be opened only in the presence of the inmate, staff may treat as general correspondence and may open, inspect, and read the mail.

You may obtain a copy of this instruction sheet from your Counselor.

All letters mailed through the Inmate's Mailbox may be opened and inspected with the exception of Legal/Special Mail.

You are cautioned that you are totally responsible for all the contents of your letters.

Incoming Packages:

Only release clothing and authorized medical devices will be authorized as incoming packages. A Request Authorization to receive package or property, BP331(58), will be prepared for all incoming packages. A Request Authorization to Mail Inmate Package, BP-Mail-17, will be prepared for all outgoing packages.

Any package received by the U.S. Post Office for which a permit has not been issued, will be rejected and returned to the sender as an unapproved package.

Outgoing Packages:

The Mail Room Officer will process outgoing inmate packages. Inmates wishing to mail out packages must bring the unsealed package to their Correctional Counselor (or authorized Unit Staff Member) in order that the contents may be checked and Form BP-Mail-17, Requesting Authorization to Mail Inmate Package, may be prepared (Attachment No. 9). The inmate must provide postage stamps required for mailing packages.

Incoming Publications:

You may make arrangements to purchase newspapers or magazines, or one of your correspondents may submit a subscription in your behalf.

You may receive hardcover books and newspapers only from the publisher, book club, or from a bookstore. You may receive soft cover material, paperback books, magazines, and newspaper clippings, from any source. You should speak with your Correctional Counselor to ascertain whether an individual issue of a publication is likely to be approved.

Reading materials that are not received from these sources will be returned to the sender.

Correspondence:

With some exception, you may write to anyone you choose. You are not authorized to write inmates in other institutions unless you have received special clearance, which is processed by your Case Manager. Depending on your institution's rules and policies it may or may not be necessary for you to submit a list of persons with whom you wish to correspond.

You may send correspondence by Registered, Certified, or Insured Mail, and may request a return receipt by placing the required postage stamps on same. Postage stamps, in different denominations can be purchased through the inmate commissary.

You may not be provided with such services as Express Mail, C.O.D., private carriers, or stamp collecting.

Telephone Calls

Inmate Telephone System

Everything you need to know about prison inmate telephone calls is below. Inmates at state institutions may have a different type of telephone system in use but it should be similar to the BOP's.

Soon after you arrive at prison or camp you will be required to sign an Acknowledgement Form stating that you understand that your telephone calls will be monitored and recorded. If you refuse to sign the Acknowledgement Form you will not be allowed to use the telephone at anytime during the length of your incarceration. I have never heard of an inmate refusing to sign the agreement.

Expect a delay of a few days to a week before your telephone privileges become active.

Don't say anything on the telephone that you don't want the Institution's Staff hearing.

The Institution's Staff are especially interested in new inmate's telephone conversations. Remember, everything you say on the institution telephone is being monitored and/or recorded. Don't be stupid and say something that will bring you heat. You would be surprised at the number of inmates who get their telephone privileges suspended for 6 months because of what they said on the telephone. Don't think you will pull one over on the staff by talking in a different language. They will have it interpreted. The use of codes on the telephone will not be allowed and will result in the immediate suspension of your telephone privileges.

Regardless if it's the truth or a lie, don't tell your family or friends on the telephone that you have been in fights with other inmates.

Don't even say that you saw inmates fighting, unless you want to be asked questions by the staff. Very few things will get you investigated faster than mentioning fighting on the telephone.

Expect long lines for the telephone, especially in the evening hours, weekends, and on holidays. If your family or friends are expecting you to call at a certain time of the day, then I would advise you to tell them to be flexible.

It is much cheaper for your family or a friend to deposit funds into your Inmate Account, for you to pay for the telephone call, than it is to make a collect call. Most first time inmates are depressed and lonely, and they can put a huge financial burden on their family and friends by making a lot of collect calls. Your first couple of months in prison will find you very depressed, and you will want to call home every 2 hours. Try to resist this urge, especially if you are calling collect.

Do not allow another inmate to talk to whomever you are talking with on the telephone for any reason. This will get you a shot and a telephone privilege suspension.

Only one-on-one telephone conversations are allowed. You are not allowed to call someone and have someone else who is there pick up an extension line to join in on the conversation.

All inmates will complete a Telephone Number Request Form before any telephone calls, either direct or collect, will be allowed. Only telephone calls made to the approved person(s) on the inmate's telephone calling list will be allowed. Simply put, if you try to call any other telephone number besides what is on your approved list, it won't go through. This form is available in the library and will have to be resubmitted for any new additions you wish to make to your telephone-calling list. Submitting more than 30 numbers for your list will require approval of the Associate Warden.

The following is taken from an Inmate's Admission and Orientation Handbook that is given to all new inmates when they arrive at prison or camp. This particular handbook was given out at the Federal Prison Camp located in Ashland, Kentucky. While some of these rules and regulations will differ slightly from prison/camp to prison/camp it should give you a good idea of what to expect.

Telephones

You have the privilege of open telephone communications. You are responsible for the content of your call. Any illegal use of the telephone system will be referred to the appropriate Law Enforcement Agency. Any unauthorized use of the telephone may result in disciplinary action.

1. Telephones are located in Building 300, across from the Commissary. You are expected to respect the privacy of others and maintain a normal voice level.
2. The telephone room is open from 6:00 a.m. to 11:30 p.m. daily. You will not be relieved from your work detail to make a phone call, except in an emergency. Your Unit Team must approve the emergency phone call.
3. All calls can either be paid for by the inmate or collect calls.
4. Telephone conversations are limited to 15 minutes.
5. No third party, credit card, conference or speakerphone calls are authorized.
6. In the event of an emergency, Staff reserves the right to temporarily suspend telephone privileges.
7. **Monitoring of Telephone Call: All calls placed from the inmate telephone room are monitored.** Contact your Correctional Counselor for specifics regarding Attorney calls.
8. Emergency calls can be made through your Correctional Counselor. After hours, contact the Shift Lieutenant.
9. No smoking or eating is permitted in the telephone room. It is your responsibility to keep the phone room clean. Abusing these rules may result in the curtailment of your telephone privileges.

The following is taken directly from an Inmate Telephone System Handout Sheet given to all new inmates when they arrive at prison or camp. This particular handout was given out at the Federal Prison Camp located in Ashland, KY. While some of these rules and regulations will differ slightly from prison/camp to prison/camp it should give you a good idea of what to expect.

The Inmate Telephone System (ITS-II) has been installed in your facility. This system allows you to place collect calls as well as direct dial calls. You will be able to place 300 minutes of calls per month. Calls will not exceed 15 minutes and you will have to wait one hour before placing your next call. Procedures for making these calls are outlined in your ITS-II Guide and printed with your new PAC.

The following briefly outlines some of the operational aspects and features of the new calling program.

- You will receive a Phone Access Code (PAC) associated with ITS-II.

- You will now transfer your funds, as well as several other functions, via the telephone keypad. This is referred to as "Telephone Teller" system. Information on the use of the "Telephone Teller" is outline in the ITS-II Guide and will be used with your PAC number.

- When making a telephone call, the called party will receive a voice message in either English or Spanish (which you will select) providing them with the following information/announcements:

    1. The type of calls being placed, either direct dial or collect.
    2. If the call is collect, the called party will be provided with the per minute rate of that call.
    3. An announcement stating, "this call is from a Federal Prison."
    4. (Your Name

5. The option to accept or deny this call or any future calls of this type.

- The local calling area will be equal to the local payphone area at your institution.
- Direct dial rates are posted in the institution law library.

ITS-II Direct Telephone Call Rates
June 18, 2004

Call Type	Per Minute Rate	July 6th Rates
Direct Dial - Local Calls	$.06	$.06
Direct Dial - Long Distance	$.20	$.23
Direct Dial - Canada	$.35	$.30
Direct Dial - Mexico	$.55	$.55
Direct Dial International	$.99	$.99

*The local calling area will be equal to the payphone calling area as defined by the Public Utilities Commission. This may cause some calls previously called local to become long distance.

Collect Call Rates (effective March 1, 2001)

State-To-State	$3.95 for the first minute $.40 for each additional minute
Interstate calls made within the State and in the local calling area	$3.81 for the first minute $.71 for each additional minute
Interstate calls made within the State and in the local calling area	$3.36 for the first minute $.13 for each additional minute
0 - 22 miles	$3.46 for the first minute $.13 for each additional minute
23 - 55 miles	$3.72 for the first minute $.41 for each additional minute
56 - 124 miles	$3.80 for the first minute $.45 for each additional minute
Local Collect Calls	$3.00 for a fifteen minute call

*The above collect rates are to be used as a guide only. Rates may vary from state to state. Rates are subject to change.

Revised March 21, 2001 "118" Balances and Options

All balances and options will be given to an inmate after dialing "118" and his Phone Access Code (PAC). The inmate will be given a list of menu options. All responses shall be spoken to the inmate in the language selected (English or Spanish only), using the Telephone Request Form.

Inmate: Dials 118 from ITS-II Telephone in his Housing Unit.

System: Provides response "enter PAC number now" (the

system shall be capable of accepting the PAC digits simultaneously while providing the voice messaging.

Inmate: Enters PAC

System: Provides menu options:
"Press 1 FOR YOU'RE "ITS BALANCE"
"Press 2 FOR YOUR COMMISSARY BALANCE"
"Press 3 TO TRANSFER FUNDS"
"Press 4 TO HEAR COST OF LAST CALL"
"Press 5 FOR NUMBERS OF CALL MINUTES REMAINING"

Upon selection by an inmate the individual processes will be as follows:

#1 For your ITS Account Balance
A) System: "your ITS Account Balance is (amount)"

#2 For your Commissary Balance
A) System: "your Commissary Balance is (amount)"

#3 To transfer funds
A) System: "your ITS Account Balance is (amount), your Commissary Account Balance is (amount). Enter the amount in whole dollars which you would like to transfer to your telephone account, followed by the # sign. Press 1 to confirm the amount." Both new balances are announced.

#4 The cost of your last call
A) System: "the cost of your last call is (amount)'

#5 For the number of call minutes remaining –

A) System: "press #5 for call minutes remaining"
"Press #3 for MONTH
"Press #2 for TOTAL MINUTES

REMAINING

*THIS CHANGE IS A RESULT OF THE 300-MINUTE LIMITATIONS. SELECTING OTHER OPTIONS SUCH AS COLLECT CALL MINUTES REMAINING OR DIRECT DIAL MINUTES REMAINING WILL GIVE INACCURATE INFORMATION BECAUSE ALL TELEPHONE CALLS ARE TRACKED TOGETHER AND THEY WILL NO LONGER BE TRACKED INDIVIDUALLY IN THE ITS-II SYSTEM AS OF APRIL 2, 2001

INMATE DIALING INSTRUCTIONS

To access your telephone account information and transfers, dial 118 and follow the instructions.

To place a local call:

- Debit: Dial the 10-digit number then your PAC.
- Collect: Dial a 0 and then the 10-digit number and finally your PAC.

To place a long distance call:

- Debit: Dial a 1 and then the 10-digit number and finally your PAC.
- Collect: Dial a 0 and then the 10-digit number and finally your PAC.

To place an International Call:

- Debit: Dial 011 and then the country and city codes plus the number and finally your PAC.
- Collect: To call International Collect, you must first make a debit call to the party and inform them to call US 888-832-3267 to have them establish an International Collect account. After the account is established (normally 2 - 4 weeks), you will be able to call International Collect to the party establishing the account. Until the time the account is established, your International Collect call will be

denied.

- After the International Collect account is established: To dial International Collect: Dial a 01 and then the country and city codes plus the number and your PAC.

Visits

Visiting Regulations

Upon your arrival at the institution you will be provided with an Initial Visiting Form. You are to list proposed relatives and friends that you wish to visit you while confined at the facility. Proposed visits that can be verified by your Correctional Counselor through your PSI or other documentation in your central file will be added to your Initial Visiting List, provided there is no questionable information.

When questionable or no information is available on a potential visitor, visiting may be denied pending receipt of background information. Visiting lists are limited to immediate family (mother, father, step-parents, foster parents, brothers, sisters, spouse and children) plus 10 other individuals. Additions and deletions to this list are to be requested at your regularly scheduled Program Review. If you have your scheduled Program Review, you may submit the visiting changes on an Inmate Request to Staff Member (cop-out). You are allowed six (6) regularly scheduled visits per month, including holiday visits.

All visitors must provide sufficient identification for staff to ensure positive identity. This identification should be a picture I.D. type i.e., a driver's license or similar identification with the individual's picture.

All visitors will enter through the Front Entrance. Each visitor will report directly to the Visiting Room Officer and complete a Visitor's Registration Form indicating they are aware of visiting regulations and they have no prohibited items on their person. After completion of this form and confirmation that the prospective visitor is on your approved Visiting List, the visitor will be directed to an area where they may wait your arrival. All visitors **Including Infants and Children** must be on the approved visiting list prior to registration.

All visitors will be subject to a search of their personal items. Only clear plastic handbags will be permitted in the visiting room. For visitors with small children, only those items necessary for the care and maintenance of the child will be permitted. Any surplus clothing, toys, etc., should remain in their car.

Any excessive display of affection between you and your visitor could result in termination of your visit. All visitors will dress appropriately and in good taste. Any visitor not in compliance will not be allowed to visit. **(Reasonable hugging and kissing at the beginning and end of visitation is acceptable.)**

Visitors are responsible for the behavior of their children. You also share the responsibility. Disorderly or disruptive behavior will not be tolerated. An adult member of the family must accompany children under the age of 16. **Failure to control the behavior of your children could result in the termination of your visit.**

Food and refreshments can be purchased from vending machines located within the visiting area. Visitors may not bring food items into the visiting room. You are expected to maintain a clean and sanitary area. Any visitor who elects to depart the area for lunch or any reason may do so, however, the visit will be terminated at that time for the remainder of the day.

No radios, cameras, tape recorders, mp3 players, or TV's are permitted in the visiting area.

You are not authorized to receive any items from a visitor or give any item to a visitor. Any authorized items will be obtained through the mail only.

You or your visitors are not to rearrange the furniture.

You are only allowed to wear your issued institution clothing in the visiting area with the exception of the white Rockport shoes sold in the Commissary. No sweat suits or shorts are allowed. All clothes must be cleaned, neatly pressed and presentable. You are only allowed to take the following items into the visiting area with you.

- Plain handkerchief
- Prescription glasses
- Comb
- Any prescribed medications which must be taken during the visit
- One religious medal with chain

You are not permitted to wear tennis shoes during a visit.

You will not be allowed to take anything from the visiting room that was not brought in with you. You are subject to search at any time and will be searched upon entering and leaving the visiting room.

You will be notified of your visit via the paging system. Do not report to the visiting area until paged. When paged, report directly to the Visiting Room Officer. You must bring your Commissary ID Card with you! When your visit ends report directly to the Visiting Room Officer for checkout.

You are to use the restroom in the visiting room restroom designated for Inmates Only. Separate facilities are provided for visitors and handicapped individuals. If you are found in a restroom other that that marked for inmate use, you will face disciplinary action.

No pets allowed within the boundaries of the institution. Pets will not be left unattended in vehicles.

Visitors are asked to leave all prescribed medication of a non-emergency nature in their vehicles. Emergency medication will be left with the Visiting Room Officer and may be obtained at any time.

The Visiting Room Officer will not accept any money or packages on your behalf.

Smoking is prohibited.

Health Care

Policy: It is the policy of the BOP that all inmates who wish to attend sick call will be allowed to do so. It is your responsibility, when desiring routine medical attention, to report to the clinic at the assigned times on the day you are to be seen. Unless you have an appointment or a medical emergency, the Health Services Department is **"Out Of Bounds"**.

Availability: Sick call is conducted on Monday, Tuesday, Wednesday, and Friday (excluding holidays).

Hours of sick call sign up are: Requests must be turned in by 7:15 a.m. Monday, Tuesday, Wednesday, and Friday.

Appointment times for sick call will be given for later in the day that you sign up for sick call, or at a later date at the discretion of the Physician Assistant present at sick call sign up.

Pill Line: You must bring your ID card and present it to pick up your medications. Pill Line is conducted daily.

Emergencies will be seen anytime.

If you should become injured or ill while on the job, notify your Detail Supervisor. Action will be taken to have you seen in the clinic.

Initial Medical Data Forms: when you arrive at the institution, a Physician's Assistant (PA) will interview you. The initial medical data forms will be completed: BP-36, Report of Medical History, and BP-Med-23, Intake Screening Form.

It is imperative that you cooperate with the PA's in supplying all requested data. This information is needed in the determination of your medical needs, establishing duty status, and assignments.

If you are on maintenance medications, these will be continued until you can be evaluated at the next routine sick call. You will be scheduled to see the PA for final determination of your medication needs.

Admission Physical: An admission physical will be completed within 7-14 days after your arrival.

If you are transferred from another BOP facility, a physical examination will not be required, providing one has been done within the past two years.

The physicals will include, but not limited to the following:

1. Hands-on physical
2. Urinalysis
3. Serology (Test for Syphilis)
4. PPD Skin Test (Tuberculosis)
5. Tetanus Toxoid
6. Dental Examination
7. EKG (age 50 and older)
8. Hearing and vision screening

If you refuse any medical screening for infectious diseases, you will be placed in Administrative Detention until all requirements have been completed. After completion of your physical examination, you will be assigned a medical duty status. This is determined by Health Services Staff and can only be changed by that department.

Biannual Physical: If you have been in the Federal Prison System for two (2) years or within two (2) months of release, you can request an update physical examination.

Duty Status:

1. Quarters: You are restricted to your cube/cell except for

meals and Health Services appointments.
2. Medically Unassigned: No work to be performed, with full recreation restriction, including hobby craft. No participating in any community activities.
3. Convalescence: Confined to unit except for meals, clinic, religious services, or visiting.

Thos individuals who require long-term chronic care will be referred to Federal Medical Facilities in Springfield, Missouri, or Rochester, Minnesota.

Dental Sick Call/Emergencies: Dental sick call sign-up is conducted Wednesday and Thursday at the clinic by appointment only. All new commitments will receive a routine examination within 14 days of your arrival at the institution. You will be informed of your dental needs, and of the manner in which routine and emergency care may be sought.

If you should develop a dental emergency during working hours, you should inform your Detail Supervisor who will take action to have you evaluated. Emergencies include those procedures for immediate relief of pain and removal of acute infection, which endangers the health of the patient.

Dental emergencies after regular clinic hours should be addressed to your Unit Officer who will take action to have you evaluated.

Education Department

1. All inmates who do not have a confirmed high school diploma or GED certificate are required to participate in the Bureau of Prison's Literacy Program (BOP Policy 5350.25, date November 3, 1997).

D.C. Code offenders in BOP custody who committed their offenses before August 5, 2000 and completed designated education programs successfully while in BOP custody on or after August 5, 1997 are eligible to receive Educational Good Time Sentence Credit. If you believe you may be eligible for Educational Good Time Sentence Credit, send a cop-out stating such to the Supervisor of Education. He/She will research your transcript, sending the paperwork to the Records Department, who will notify you of the amount, if any, of earned GCT.

2. All inmates incarcerated in the BOP must be able to read and write the English Language with a degree of proficiency. This proficiency is measured through the Comprehensive Adult Student Assessment Systems or CASAS Test. Students who do not score a minimum of 225 on the CASAS Test are required to participate in the English as a Second Language (ESL) Program. When the ESL Program is successfully completed, a $25.00 cash award and a certificate are given.

3. Inmates who do not possess a GED or a high school diploma are required to take the Adult Basic Learning examination (ABLE). For those students who speak the Spanish Language the SABE Test will be administered. Inmates must spend a minimum of 240 hours in the Literacy Program or until a GED is achieved, whichever comes first. For students subject to the Violent Crime Control Law Enforcement Act (VCCLEA) or the Prison Litigation Reform Act (PLRA), failure to make satisfactory progress toward a GED credential may affect the awarding of Good Conduct Time (GCT). When the GED Program is successfully completed, a $25.00 cash

award and a certificate are given.

4. All inmates who are required to participate in the GED or ESI Programs must attend the designated classes held each weekday.

5. Institutional clothing must be worn in the Educational Department during the normal working day (7:30 a.m. until 4:00 p.m.). Casual clothing may be worn during off-duty hours and on weekends, but it must be within the bounds of good taste. Shirts and shoes must be worn at all times, and tank tops are not permitted.

6. No radios or food are allowed in the Educational Department.

7. Students are not authorized to leave the Educational Department for any reason, other than for a call-out or designated breaks.

8. Inmates may use the library areas during their off-duty hours. Inmates caught in the department during their on-duty hours will receive an incident report and a suspension of library privileges.

9. Inmates may not enter the area designated for the library clerk. Both library areas are open from 8:00 a.m. until 9:30 p.m. everyday.

10. Law books and other materials may not be removed from the department for any reason. A variety of books are available from the library, and the Inter-Loan Book Program is offered through local public libraries.

11. Adult continuing Education Courses are offered by the Department. Offerings include foreign languages, business courses, history, art, etc.

Parenting Program:

The Parenting Program is designed to provide parenting skills to the inmate population with children. The program will help the student to assess family values, goals, and skills as a parent while learning other styles and techniques of parenting. Interaction visits are offered quarterly for those enrolled in the program.

Pre-Release and Career Counseling:

The Education Department conducts several classes which fall under an inmate's pre-release programming. Classes such as Resume Writing, Finding Jobs, Interviewing Skills, Money Management, Credit & Loans, and Bank Accounts are offered. Inmates with Career Counseling needs can participate in a self-help program, which assists them with career planning and development.

Drug Abuse Programs & Psychology Groups

During Admission and Orientation a short orientation to the services offered through the Psychology Department will be presented. Psychology Services offer individual and group therapy, as well as the Drug Treatment Program. After A&O is completed, individuals will be screened via a call-out or by being paged to the Psychology Services Office.

Drug Abuse Education:

Drug Abuse Education is a 30-hour class taught by the Drug Abuse Treatment Specialist. The class teaches about drugs, addiction, recovery, and meets several times a week. At the end of the 30 hours, participants must pass a written test with a 70% and they will receive a Certificate of Completion. Many inmates are required to take the class in accordance with BOP policies. If you are required, you will be contacted when your time comes to begin the class. However, every inmate is encouraged to volunteer to take the class.

Drug Abuse Treatment:

The Non-Residential Drug Treatment Program is designed to meet the needs of recovering addicts and alcoholics. The program is open to all inmates who volunteer and who are recovering from drug/alcohol addictions. Treatment is designed to help recovering addicts develop sobriety plans and change drug-centered lifestyles. The program consists of a variety of activities such as group psychotherapy, counseling, homework assignments, classroom lectures, etc. Each participant will develop and agree to an individual treatment plan. These treatment plans are developed by the inmate and his Treatment Counselor and may include participation in other psychology groups such as Stress

Management, Anger Management, General Psychotherapy, or the Parenting Program.

Transitional Service:

Transitional Services are provided to any inmate who has successfully completed a BOP Residential Drug Treatment Program at other institutions. Services provide aftercare counseling while an inmate is at their institution, as well as, assistance to Unit Staff for setting up Drug Treatment Services at Community Correction Centers after an inmate's release.

Psychology Groups:

There are a number of groups, classes and services offered by the Psychologists in Psychology Services. Send a cop-out to Psychology Services to inquire about the availability of the following groups:

Audio Tape Self-Help Library:

A variety of audiotapes are available for listening. These self-help tapes cover topics that inspire and assist the listener in self-improvement efforts. The tapes and tape players will be issued on an individual basis and are to be used in the Psychology Services area <u>only.</u>

Special Topic Groups:

The following groups are available as needs arise and time permits.

1. Breaking Barriers
2. Living Free
3. Alcoholics Anonymous/Narcotics Anonymous
4. Smart Recovery
5. Relapse Prevention
6. Beat the Street

Watch the Unit Bulletin Board for group announcements or contact Psychology Services for updated information.

Breaking Barriers

The Breaking Barriers group is a 20-hour program designed to help participants:

- Identify major barriers of thinking which diminish the possibility of positive change.
- Develop positive alternatives.
- Establish goals to overcome barriers.
- Develop positive coping strategies.

Living Free

The Living Free group is a 20-hour group designed to help participants:

- Look at the cost of criminal lifestyle.
- Learn to recognize thoughts that support a faulty lifestyle.
- Learn how to change and maintain new habits.
- Identify how current lifestyle adversely affects family and community.
- Develop a positive plan to change.

Alcoholics Anonymous/Narcotics Anonymous:

Alcoholics Anonymous/Narcotics Anonymous, while not considered therapy or treatment, is important adjuncts to treatment for individuals with alcohol and drug related problems. As such, they may be recommended by Drug Treatment Staff, and therefore, constitute a component of the Non-Residential Drug Treatment Program. These groups are also held weekly for the Spanish-speaking inmates.

Smart Recovery:

This is an alternate support program for substance abuse problems. It is based on the principal of rational emotive therapy. An inmate, co-facilitated by a staff member, leads this group.

Relapse Prevention "Living Sober":

The Living Sober Relapse Prevention Group is a 16-week program designed to help participants:

- Resist social pressures to use chemicals.
- Cope with cravings and thoughts of using.
- Manage anger.
- Manage feelings of boredom and emptiness.
- Cope with family and inter-personal conflict.
- Build a recovery network and sponsorship.
- Cope with relapse warning signs and high-risk situations.

"Beat the Street" Recovery Program:

Beat the Street Group is a 20-week recovery program designed to help participants:

- Learn to avoid relapse.
- Cope with unsupportive family members.
- Use support systems.
- Make housing plans before leaving prison.
- Prepare to handle the inevitable triggers and cravings.
- Men's issues in early recovery.
- Coping with the stress of parenting in recovery.
- Coping with emotions such as anger, guilt, shame, and self-pity.
- Having fun clean and sober.
- Getting a job and keeping it.
- Reclaiming long-term dreams.

Inmate Suicide Companion Training/Cadre Participation:

Inmates are trained to be "suicide watch companions" for inmates who have been placed on suicide watch. Inmates who are interested should send a cop-out to Psychology Services.

Inmates should notify staff when they have reason to believe another inmate may be suicidal.

Religious Activities

The Religious Services Department provides for your spiritual needs regardless of your religious affiliation. The department also assists in the correctional process to the fullest extent possible.

The Chaplain maintains a flexible program for all religious faiths, which includes general and private worship, Bible study, spiritual development, group discussions, classes and meditation. The schedule of activities is posted on your Unit Bulletin Board.

The Chaplin's work schedule has been designed to meet any of your special needs when they arise. Their schedule includes evenings.

Inmates are free to find their own way of participation.

The Chaplain is available to any seeking assistance in finding solutions to problems, direction for decisions, and perspective in their circumstances.

Note: If you wish to be married, you must receive permission from the Warden. Anyone contemplating marriage should contact the Chaplain and your Case Manager. Your Case Manager will process the request for approval for the Warden. The Chaplain will make final arrangements.

Recreation

Recreation Department

The following is an example of the recreation activities that are offered at a Federal Prison Camp. Your institution may offer more Hobby Crafts.

1. Recreation Yard: The Recreation Department currently offers the following activities:

- Basketball
- Volleyball
- Racquetball
- Paddle Tennis
- Bocce Ball
- Horseshoes
- Walking

2. Recreation Hall: Open year-round; our recreation hall affords a variety of activities for all interested inmates. Activities include:

- Billiards
- Stair Climbers
- Exercising
- Weight Lifting

3. Holidays: On all holidays, tournaments and special events are scheduled to offer a wide variety of activities to the population. Holiday Flyers are distributed and posted in the Rec. Hall showing dates, events and times of scheduled events. These flyers serve as a guide to schedule events, and are subject to change from time to time without notice.

4. Leagues: Organized leagues are run by the Recreational

Department in various sports. Check with the Recreation Specialist for more information concerning upcoming leagues.

5. **Awards:** Upon completion of league play, tournament play, the participants may be eligible for incentive awards. During all league play, players must compete in two-thirds of all scheduled events in order to receive an award. In holiday events, awards are given to first and second place finishers only. Post-season tournaments (following completion of regular season play) generally have awards for first and second place finishers.

6. **Officiating:** The Recreation Department is constantly interested in recruiting inmates to officiate in organized league play. Inmates who desire to be scorekeepers, timekeepers, umpires or referees are eligible to officiate upon meeting the following requirements:

- Be impartial and conduct yourself professionally.
- Posse's sensible judgment and good conduct.
- Be in good physical condition.
- Have the ability to read and understand rules.

7. **Hobby Craft:** At the present time, the only type of leisure hobby craft available to the population is artwork. Artwork is limited to water colors, drawing, colored pencils, etc. Due to space limitations, you are required to keep artwork or supplies in your living area. Art supplies may be purchased via special order through the Recreation Department.

7. **Equipment:** Items such as weight lifting belts, gloves, braces, wraps, etc., may be purchased through the Commissary. If you have any questions contact the Recreation Specialist.

Counts

Get ready to be counted. Inmates will be counted at least 6 times a day. Count time is considered to be a Holy Time in prison. It's when the CO's walk-thru the units counting every inmate.

Along with the regularly scheduled counts there are several other types of counts that will be announced. You should orient yourself to the time and type of each count.

During all counts, unless you are at your work detail, you are to be in your cube or cell and remain quiet. Don't even get caught whispering. No radios on and no headphones on your head. If it's a stand up count, which you will have one or two a day that are scheduled, you are to be standing by your bed. The CO's must be able to see your face when they walk past your house. No eating during the counts. Counts are not finished until you hear the CO say "Clear".

Example of Count Procedures

Official Daily Counts:	Saturday, Sunday & Holidays
Midnight	Midnight
3:00 a.m.	3:00 a.m.
5:00 a.m.	5:00 a.m.
4:00 p.m. (Stand Up Count)	10:00 a.m. (Stand Up Count)
10:00 p.m.	4:00 p.m. (Stand Up Count)
	10:00 p.m.

Other types of counts that will be called are:

Fog Counts - If it's foggy in the morning you will get one of these.

Special Count - Nothing special about it. It's just a regular count.

Emergency Count - Usually a Stand Up Count

Knuckle Count - the inmates call it this. It's when the CO's will tell everyone to take their shirts off, so they can look for cuts and bruises from a fight. They will also look at your knuckles and your lips. This is usually a Stand Up Count. This type of count occurs when an inmate has asked for medical treatment because of a fight he was in. The inmate usually won't rat on the other inmate that he was fighting with, which causes the CO's to go and look for him.

Photo Count - This is a Stand Up Count. The CO's will walk around with a book with every inmate's photo and ID number. They will match you with the photo and ask you to say your name and ID number out loud.

Census Count - This is just a regular count that may be a Stand Up Count or may not be.

Accountability - This is a regular count. Usually not a Stand Up Count.

These counts listed above can and will be called at all hours of the day and night.

Usually the CO will announce if the count is to be a Stand Up Count. The announcement will usually go something like this:

"Attention in the units. Attention on the compound.

Count Time! Count Time!

All inmates return to their cubes or cells for the 4:00 standing count.

Stand by your bunks and keep your mouths shut!"

I can't stress how important it is for you to be in your house during a count. If it's a standing count, be standing. Remain quiet until you hear the CO announce that the count has been cleared. Sometimes on weekends or holidays some inmates will sleep until the 10:00 a.m. count. Always look around and make sure no one is sleeping in the houses around you during a standing count. It's a guaranteed trip to the Hole if you are caught sleeping during a standing count.

If a count is not good there will be a recount. If the recount is not good, all hell will break loose and every CO will converge on the unit that has caused the recount.

If you are in the toilets during a night count the CO's will usually yell to see if anyone is in the toilets. If you happen to be walking back to your house from the toilets at night during a count, you should stop and stand still where you are when you see a CO counting. This will allow the CO's to count you. If you try to quickly move back to your house while they are counting you will definitely hear about it.

The evening meal is served after the 4:00 p.m. count. On weekends and holidays, brunch is served after the 10:00 a.m. count.

Guards

Guards/CO's

In prison the guards are called CO's (Correctional Officers). Like everything else, the higher the security level of the institution the tougher they get. Most of the CO's I encountered along the way were no-nonsense types who were professional and fair. They have a difficult job, and one I wouldn't want. Not every inmate will agree with me on this point, but a lot would.

Like everything else in life there are good ones and bad ones.

CO's should be given their space. Never walk up to one unless he is fully aware that you are doing so. Never walk up behind one for any reason.

Most inmates call the CO's "Boss". The inmates will call almost every CO a nickname, and it's usually one that they wouldn't call the CO's to their face.

CO's at camps, while still professional, can be a little more lenient then those working behind the fence.

Shots

Shots, or Tickets, are written reprimands that inmates receive for infractions of the rules. If you receive an excessive amount of shots you will receive raised sanctions.

Inmate Extortion & Prohibited Acts

Inmate Extortion

Extortion happens in prison just as it happens out in the world. Most times it is violence or sexual assault that gets threatened. This is why you should never tell anyone about you or your family's financial situation. Extortion at the lower level security institutions is rare (I never heard of even one instance), but this is good information for you to know.

When you first arrive you will, in time, be questioned by other inmates about your background. This is not to say that they will try to extort money from you, some inmates are simply bored and curious. But a good rule is to always use caution when you tell other inmates about your family, and never tell them about your financial situation. Even your celly shouldn't know too much about your financial situation.

The following is an example of a hustle that might try to be played at the higher security level institutions. A seasoned inmate who has served time at every security level of institution told this example to me.

One type of extortion hustle that might get played on first time inmates is the good guy bad guy routine. Soon after a new inmate arrives a hostile and aggressive inmate that will threaten him with violence, if he doesn't pay protection money each month will accost him. At this point a second inmate, who has already met and got to know the new inmate, will come to the rescue. He will tell the aggressive inmate to back off and leave the new inmate alone. This usually impresses the new inmate and he feels safe around that inmate. The good guy inmate will then suggest to the new inmate that if he will pay him each month that he will see to it that no one else bothers him. He won't call it paying protection money but instead will tell a tale of being poor and needy. The new inmate, believing that he is helping a new friend, and at the same time ensuring his own safety, will agree. That money will be split between that inmate and the aggressive inmate, who were partners from the start.

If this happens to you and you find yourself being threatened with violence you will have to decide what the best course of action to take is. Some inmate's pay and others won't. Some will go to the CO's and ask to be put into segregation for their own safety. The CO's will want to know why and will launch an investigation. This will put you in the position of being labeled a snitch. I won't attempt to tell you what you should do if you find yourself in the position of being extorted.

Of course the higher up your institution's security level is the more extortion you will find. Most of these inmates are serving 30 plus years to life, and they really don't care if they get caught trying to extort money. This is another popular gang related hustle that, if you are going to that higher level of institution, you will probably soon experience or hear about.

My best advice is for you to try and avoid the gangs, drugs, sex, alcohol, and cigarettes, gambling, stealing or borrowing. These are the 8 sins in prison that will get you nothing but trouble. Most inmates will tell you that if you mind your own business, respect other inmates, and don't look like you have money you will be all right.

Prohibited Acts & Disciplinary Severity Scale

Greatest Category

Read over these Prohibited Acts and Sanctions. This will give you a good idea of what type of sanctions can, and will be imposed against you if you violate any of the institution's rules or policies. Remember, no violation goes unpunished!

Code & Prohibited Acts (High Category)

100 Killing.

101 Assaulting any Person (Including Sexual Assault) or an Armed Assault on the institutions' secure perimeter (a charge for assaulting).

102 Escape from Escort, Escape from a secure institution (Security Level 2 through 6 and administrative institutions); or Escape from a Security Level 1 institution with violence.

103 Setting a Fire (charged with this act in this category only when found to pose a threat to life or a threat of serious bodily harm or in furtherance of a prohibited act of greatest severity, e.g., in furtherance of a riot or escape; otherwise the charge is properly classified Code 218 or 329).

104 Possession, Manufacture, or Introduction of a Gun, Firearm, Weapon, Sharpened Instrument, Knife, Dangerous Chemical, Explosive or any Ammunition.

105 Rioting

106 Encouraging Others to Riot

107 Taking Hostages

Sanctions:

A. Recommend Parole date rescission or retardation.

B. Forfeit earned Statutory Good Time (up to 100%) and/or terminate or disallow Extra Good Time (an Extra Good Time sanction may not be suspended).

B1. Disallow ordinarily between 50% & 75% (27 – 41 days) of Good Conduct Time credit available for year (a Good Conduct Time sanction may not be suspended).

C. Disciplinary Transfer (Recommended)

D. Disciplinary Segregation (Up to 60 Days)

E. Make Monetary Restitution

F. Withhold Statutory Good Time (Note – can be in addition to A through E) – cannot be the only sanction executed.

G. Loss of privileges (Note – can be in addition to A through E) cannot be the only sanction executed.

Code & Prohibited Acts (High Category)

108 Possession, Manufacture, or Introduction of a Hazardous Tool (tool most likely to be used in an Escape or Escape Attempt or to serve as weapons capable of doing serious bodily harm to others; or those hazardous to institutional security of personal safety; e.g., hacksaw blade).

109 Refusing to Provide a Urine Sample or take part in other drug-abuse testing.

110 Introduction of any narcotics, or related paraphernalia not prescribed for the individual by the medical staff.

111 Use of any narcotics, or related paraphernalia not prescribed for the individual by the medical staff.

112 Possession of any narcotics, or related paraphernalia not prescribed for the individual by the medical staff.

113 Use of the telephone to further criminal activity (greatest severity).

114 Interfering with a Staff Member in Performance of Duties. (Conduct must be of the greatest severity nature.) This charge is to be used only when another charge or greatest severity is not applicable.

115 Conduct with disrupts or interferes with the security or orderly running of the institution or the Bureau of Prisons. (Conduct must be of the greatest severity nature.) This charge is to be used only when another charge of greatest severity is not applicable.

Sanctions:

Sanctions A – G

Code & Prohibited Acts (High Category)

200 Escape from Unescorted Community Programs and Activities and Open Institutions (Security Level 1) and from Outside Security Institutions without violence.

201 Fighting with Another Person.

202 Threatening Another with Bodily Harm or any other offense.

203 Extortion, Blackmail, Protection: demanding or receiving money or anything of value in return for protection against others, to avoid bodily harm, or under threat of informing.

204 Engaging in Sexual Acts.

205 Making Sexual Proposals or Threats To Another.

206 Wearing a Disguise or a Mask.

207 Possession of any Unauthorized Locking Devise, or lock pick, or tampering with or blocking any lock device (including keys), or destroying, altering, interfering with, improperly using, or damaging any security device, mechanism, or procedure.

208 Adulteration of any Food or Drink.

209 (Not to be Used)

210 Possessing any Staff's Clothing

Sanctions:

A. Recommend Parole date Rescission or Retardation.

B. Forfeit earned Statutory Good Time up to 50% or up to 60 days, whichever is less, and/or terminate or disallow Extra Good Time (An Extra Good Time sanction may not be suspended.)

C. Disciplinary Transfer (Recommended).

D. Disciplinary Segregation (Up to 30 Days).

E. Make Monetary Restitution.

F. Withhold SGT

G. Loss of Privileges: Commissary, Movies, Recreation, etc.

H. Change Housing Quarters

I. Remove from Program and/or Group Activity.

J. Loss of Job.

K. Impound Inmate's Personal Property.

L. Confiscate Contraband.

M. Restrict to Quarters.

Code & Prohibited Acts (High Category)

211 Engaging in, or Encouraging a Group Demonstration.

212 Encouraging others to refuse to Work, or to participate in a Work Stoppage.

213 (Not to be Used)

214 Introduction of Alcohol into BOP Facility.

215 Giving or Offering an Official or Staff Member a Bribe, or Anything of Value.

216 Giving Money To, or Receiving Money From, any Person for Purposes of Introducing Contraband of for any other Illegal or Prohibited Purposes.

217 Destroying, Altering, or Damaging Government Property, or the Property of Another Person, having a value in excess of $100.00 or destroying, altering, or damaging life-safety devices (e.g., fire alarm) regardless of financial value.

218 Stealing (Theft; this includes data obtained through the unauthorized use of communication facility, or through the

unauthorized access of disks, tapes, or computer printouts or other automated equipment on which data is stored.

219 Demonstrating, Practicing or Using Martial Arts, Boxing (Except for use of a punching bag), Wrestling, or other forms of physical encounter, or military exercises of drill.

220 Being in an Unauthorized Area with a Person of the Opposite Sex without Staff Permission.

221 Making, Possessing, or Using Intoxicants.

222 Refusing to Breathe into a Breathalyzer or take part in other testing for use of alcohol.

223 Assaulting any Person (Charged with this act only when a less serious physical injury or contact has been attempted or carried out by an inmate.)

224 Use of the telephone for abuses other than criminal activity (e.g., circumventing telephone monitoring procedures, possession and/or use of another inmate's PIN number; third-party calling, third-party billing; using credit card numbers to place telephone calls; conference calling; talking in code) High Severity.

225 Interfering with a Staff Member in the Performance of Duties. (Conduct must be of the high severity nature.) This charge is to be used only when another charge of high severity is not applicable.

226 Conduct which Disrupts or Interferes with the Security or Orderly Running of the Institution or the BOP. (Conduct must be of the high severity nature.) This charge is to be used only when another charge of high severity is not applicable.

Sanctions:

Sanctions A – M

Code & Prohibited Acts (Moderate Category)

300 Indecent Exposure

301 (Not to be Used)

302 Misuse of Authorized Medication

303 Possession of Money or Currency, unless specifically authorized, or in excess of the amount authorized.

304 Loaning of Property of anything of value for profit or increased return.

305 Possession of Anything Not Authorized for Retention or Receipt by the inmate, and not issued to him through regular channels.

306 Refusing to Work or to Accept a Program Assignment.

307 Refusing to Obey an Order by any Staff Member (may be categorized and charged in terms of greater severity, according to the nature of the order being disobeyed; e.g., Failure to Obey an Order which furthers a riot would be charged as 105, Rioting, Refusing to Obey an Order which furthers a fight would be charged as 201, Fighting; Refusing to Provide a Urine Sample when ordered, would be charged as 110).

308 Violating a Condition of a Furlough.

309 Violating a Condition of a Community Program.

310 Unexcused Absence from Work or an Assignment.

311 Failure to Perform Work as Instructed by the Supervisor.

312 Insolence toward a Staff Member.

313 Lying or Providing a False Statement to a Staff Member.

314 Counterfeiting, Forging or Unauthorized Reproduction of Any Document, Article of Identification, Money, Security, or Official Paper. (May be categorized in terms of greater severity according to the nature of the item being reproduced; e.g., counterfeiting release papers to effect escape, Code 102 or Code 200).

315 Participating in an Unauthorized Meeting or Gathering.

316 Being in an Unauthorized Area.

317 Failure to Follow Safety Sanitation Regulations.

318 Using any Equipment or Machinery, which is not Specifically Authorized.

319 Using any Equipment or Machinery Contrary to Instructions or Posted Safety Standards.

320 Failure to Stand Count.

321 Interfering with the Taking of Count.

322 (Not to be Used)

323 (Not to be Used)

324 Gambling

325 Preparing or Conducting a Gambling Pool.

326 Possession of Gambling Paraphernalia.

327 Unauthorized Contacts with the Public.

328 Giving Money or Anything of Value to or Accepting Money or Anything of Value from: another inmate or any other person without staff authorization.

329 Destroying, altering, or damaging government property, or the property of another person, having a value of $100.00 or less.

330 Being Unsanitary or Untidy; failing to keep ones person and one's quarters in accordance with posted standards.

331 Possession, Manufacture, or Introduction of a Non-Hazardous Tool or other Non-Hazardous Contraband (Tool not likely to be used in an escape or escape attempt, or to serve as a weapon capable of doing seriously bodily harm to others, or not hazardous to institutional security or personal safety; other non-hazardous contraband includes such items as food or cosmetics).

332 Smoking

397 Use of the telephone for abuses other than criminal activity (e.g., conference calling; possession and/or use of another inmate's PIN number; three-way calling; providing false information for preparation of a telephone list) (moderate severity)

398 Interfering with a Staff Member in the Performance of Duties. (Conduct must be of the moderate severity nature.) This charge of moderate severity is not applicable.

399 Conduct which Disrupts or Interferes with the Security or Orderly Running of the Institution or the BOP. (Conduct

must be of the moderate severity nature.) This charge of moderate severity is not applicable.

Sanctions:

Sanctions A – N

Code & Prohibited Acts (Low Moderate Category)

400 Possession of Property Belonging to another Person.

401 Possession Unauthorized Amount of Otherwise Authorized Clothing.

404 Using Abusive or Obscene Language

405 Tattooing or Self-Mutilation

407 Conduct with a Visitor in Violation of Bureau Regulations (Restriction or loss for a specific period of time, of these privileges may often be an appropriate sanction G)

408 Conducting a Business

409 Unauthorized Physical Contact (e.g., kissing, embracing)

Sanctions

B.1 Disallow Ordinarily up to 12.5% of Good Conduct Time credit available for year (to be used only where inmate found to have committed a second violation of the same prohibited act within 6 months); disallow ordinarily up to 25% (1 – 15 days) of GCT credit available for year (to be used only where inmate found to have committed a third violation of the same prohibited act within 6 months) (A GCT Time Sanction may not be suspended).

E. Make Monetary Restitution

F. Withhold Statutory Good Time

G. Loss of Privileges: Commissary, Movies, Recreation, etc.

H. Change Housing Quarters

I. Remove from Program and/or Group Activity

J. Loss of Job

K. Impound Inmate's Personal Property

L. Confiscate Contraband

M. Restrict to Quarters

N. Extra Duty

O. Reprimand

P. Warning

Code & Prohibited Acts (Low Moderate Category)

497 Use of the telephone for abuses other than criminal activity (e.g., exceeding the 15-minute time limit for telephone calls; using the telephone in an unauthorized area; placing of any unauthorized individual on the telephone list (low severity).

498 Interfering with a Staff Member in the Performance of Duties. (Conduct must be of the low moderate severity nature.) This charge is to be used only when another charge of low moderate severity is not applicable.

499 Conduct Which Disrupts or Interferes with the Security or Orderly Running of the Institution or the BOP. (Conduct must be of the low moderate severity nature.) This charge is to be used only when another charge of low moderate severity is not applicable.

Sanctions:

Sanctions B.1 – F

Sanction B.1 may be imposed in the low moderate category only where the inmate has committed the same low moderate prohibited act more than one time within a six-month period.

Aiding another person to commit any of these offenses, Attempting to commit any of these offenses, and making plans to commit any of these offenses, in all categories of severity, shall be considered the same as a commission of the offense itself.

Searches/Shakedowns

You are in prison so expect to get searched often. Searches can happen at any time and at any place. Any CO can order you to stand in the search position and search you. Inmates leaving the cafeteria are frequently searched for food items that didn't get eaten inside the cafeteria. A good rule here is don't be carrying anything around with you that you shouldn't be.

Some institutions will have shakedown shacks outside the cafeteria where inmates will have to go inside and strip down to be searched.

Shakedowns are also a daily event in most institutions. A shakedown is where one or more CO's will come into a cell/cube and search every nook and cranny. The inmates living there will be ordered to leave the cell/cube while the shakedown is taking place. The CO's are very thorough and usually don't miss anything. You can expect everything you have to be searched from your locker to your bed.

Almost every inmate has some form of contraband and usually the CO's will let the small things go, but not every time.

If, during a shakedown of your house, contraband is found in a common area of your cube/cell, both you and your celly will receive a shot or a trip to the Hole, unless one of you claim ownership of the item.

The Hole

The Hole is a block of cells in the segregation unit of the institution. It's usually the oldest, smelliest, and most rundown housing unit at the institution. The Hole is where inmates are sent for punishment, investigations, and protective custody.

Inmates in the Hole are locked down for 23 hours of the day, and are only allowed to shower twice a week. There will be a combination toilet/sink in each cell. All meals will be delivered and eaten in the cells.

There are no TV's or activities of any sort. Inmates are allowed 1 hour each day (usually in the morning) for exercise. The Hole's exercise area is a fenced area away from other inmates in general population. The Hole is good for one thing, and that is lying on your bunk and staring at the ceiling. Try doing that for 90 days!

The CO will pack out all of your personal and issued items, but your bedding stays in your room. Inmates that get sent to the Hole can expect their mattress and/or pillow to be gone when they get back. Inmates call this taking a hit. It's common knowledge among inmates that, unless you're celly holds you down, if you go to the Hole you are going to get hit.

Cop-Outs/Call-Outs

Cop-Outs

A Cop-Out is a written request from an inmate to any department or staff member. Cop-Out forms are located in the Counselor's Building and the Library.

A Cop-Out form asks for the inmate's name, register number, work assignment and unit number.

A Cop-Out form asks that the inmate briefly state their question or concern and the solution they are requesting. They may continue writing on the back of the form if they run short of room on the front. If necessary, the inmate will be interviewed in order to successfully respond to their request.

Call-Outs

Call Outs are simply inmate appointments. The Call-Out Board will tell an inmate when and where he is required to be somewhere. It may be for a dental appointment or for a meeting with a Case Manager. Call-Out Boards are centrally located at most institutions and are updated each day, Monday – Friday. Always check the Call-Out Board each day! If you miss a call out you probably will receive a reprimand.

A permanent non Call-Out bulletin board is located in each housing unit wing. You are expected to review this bulletin board daily for pertinent information, which might concern you. At no time should anything be removed from the bulletin board without prior approval from a staff member.

10-Minute Move

If you are serving your time at a low security institution, or higher, you will follow the stressful 10 Minute Move Rule. This means that inmates are only allowed to go from one location to another during the first 10 minutes of every hour.

For example, if you wanted to go to the Rec. Yard, or anywhere else, you have to wait for the 10-minute move to be called before you are allowed to leave your unit. Once there you will have to wait for the next move to be called before you can return (unless you can do what you need to do and then get back within those 10 minutes). All unit doors and the Rec. Yard gate are locked after the announcement that the move is completed. After the move if you are caught outside anywhere else but in the Rec. Yard, you will get a shot and probably a trip to the Hole.

Restricted movement like this gets worse the higher up the security institutions that you go.

Camps do not have the 10 Minute Move rule.

The Warden

The Warden is the top dog at any institution. He has the last say in any major decision that needs to be made.

Hopefully you will only see the Warden when he does a walk through. Usually an Assistant Warden will be the highest member of the staff that any inmate comes in contact with. The Warden will make his rounds, and sometimes stop and talk to inmates, but it's rare that he will have the time to talk for very long.

Most inmates give the Warden a wide berth when they see him coming. The Warden will expect to be shown respect from every inmate he comes in contact with. If you do happen to come in contact with the Warden, I would advice you to show him his respect, even if you don't mean it.

The Inmate's 10 Commandments

Here are the Inmate's 10 Commandments. If you don't learn anything else from this guidebook, learn these! These are the 10 of the most important things that you need to know in order to avoid trouble and stay safe! Learn them, know them, and live them.

1) Don't snitch, rat, or tell on anyone, about anything.

2) Don't steal from another inmate

3) Mind your own business about everything. This one is important enough to repeat. MIND YOUR OWN BUSINESS ABOUT EVERYTHING!

4) Don't look into other inmate's houses as you walk past, and never go into an inmate's house when he is not at home.

5) Don't wake up a sleeping inmate, unless it is to warn him about something that affects him.

6) Treat other inmates with respect, just as you want to be respected.

7) Don't walk around naked, or in you're "Tighty-Whities".

8) If you borrow something, pay it back when you say you are going to. But better still just don't borrow anything.

9) Shower Often - Flush Often, no one wants to smell your body or toilet funk.

10) Don't ear hustle (listening to other's conversations).

8 Sins

If you are a first time inmate, and you want to avoid the drama and just serve your time and go home, then you should avoid all of the 8 Sins in prison.

The 8 Sins in prison are gangs, drugs, sex, alcohol, cigarettes, gambling, stealing and borrowing. Prison is prison but if you have the money you can get almost anything you want. Borrowing is not quite a sin, but I included it because it causes a lot of problems when inmates don't pay back their debt. Remember, that if you just want to do your time and go home, stay away from these sins.

I included cigarettes because in 2005 the BOP decided that no inmates would be permitted to smoke. They no longer sell cigarettes, cigars or pipe tobacco in their commissaries. Rumor had it that there is also a plan to eliminate chewing tobacco and dip. If you are heading to a state joint you may still have your smoking privileges, but state prison systems usually copy the feds. Enjoy it while it lasts!

Some inmates are addicted to cigarettes and have an extremely tough time trying to break the habit. Cigarettes are smuggled into prisons and sold by inmates to those addicted. At the time of this writing, cigarettes were selling for up to $150.00 a pack. A lot of inmates will buy these cigarettes on a type of credit plan that calls for payment at a later date. If that date rolls around and the payment hasn't been made the inmate will probably receive a visit by a collector. If you smoke now, and are being sent to a federal prison in the near future, you should try and stop before you go. You will have a lot of things to worry about in prison, but going cold turkey on cigarettes shouldn't be one of them. Avoid those inmates who are selling cigarettes just as you should avoid the ones selling drugs.

It really is as simple as that. Obey the Inmate's 10 Commandments, avoid the 8 Sins, and you won't have any problems.

Other Inmates

What I'm about to write could go against everything you believe in. I know it did for me, but I have been to prison and I know how things are. If you believe that everyone should be treated equally, regardless of his or her race, religion, or sexuality choices, then you need to stop and think about it. You are going to prison. There is no "politically correctness" in prison. That's not to say that you don't give everyone his or her respect, because you do. It's just that there are some inmates that, unless you are of the same religion or belief, you avoid. Most Muslims in prison only hang with other Muslims. Rastafarians only hang with other Rastafarians. Whites usually hang with whites, and Hispanics usually hang with Hispanics. The Nation of Islam Brothers, will usually only associate with other members of The Nation. It even falls back to what state or city you are from. Inmates from Cleveland will hang with other inmates from Cleveland. Inmates from NYC will hang with other inmates from NYC, and this is sometimes regardless of race.

This will also carry over to the cafeteria. White inmates sit with white inmates, black inmates sit with black inmates, and Hispanic inmates sit with Hispanic inmates.

Exceptions are made. If you are doing business with an inmate, like buying food from him on a regular basis, then you will be friends. Hustles are hustles and any inmate, if he is getting paid, will be a friend with whoever is paying him.

I guess what I'm saying is that if you want friends in prison, you should seek out those that will share the most in common with you. It's not hard to figure out. If you are a white inmate from Tennessee you probably won't hang out with a black inmate from Harlem, New York. That's just the way it is.

Inmates in prisons come in all sizes, races and ages. You are going to be living in very tight quarters with possibly up to thousands of other men. Just like you, these men were all convicted of breaking the law and, just like you; none of these men want to be incarcerated. It is a sometimes-stressful atmosphere with a very real threat of violence that could happen at anytime and for any reason.

You should already know what type of person you are before you arrive at prison. Are you the quiet type who just wants to do your time as stress free as possible and go home? Or are you the type who likes it loud and is constantly seeking out the action and the vices, to have as much fun as you can while you are serving your stretch of time? Are you a gangbanger from the streets that will be looking to run with your brothers in prison? The type of person you are now will have a lot to do with how you do your time in prison.

I'm not trying to tell you how to do your time. You are obviously an adult and you don't need anyone telling you right from wrong. But prison life is just like life on the streets, with regard to the different types of trouble you can find. Just like on the streets, if you are looking for someone that can hook you up with drugs, and if you have the money, then you will find them. The trouble with the drugs, and the other vices that you can find in prison is, just like in the streets, you can get busted or killed. If you are a first time inmate and you want to avoid the drama and just serve your time and go home, then you should avoid all of the 8 Sins in prison.

In prison, just like anywhere else, you are going to find people who are just no damn good. These inmates just seem to attract trouble like a magnet. It won't take you long to learn who these inmates are. They are usually the inmates who are loud, and are always arguing. They don't respect other inmates, yet they get furious when they think they are being disrespected. Avoid these inmates. Almost every other inmate hates them and won't have anything to do with them.

It's hard to believe but there are grown men in prison who just won't take a shower. They stink and no one wants to get near them. I have even seen inmates writing anonymous cop-outs to the prison counselors asking them to order that inmate to take a shower. Avoid these lazy inmates.

Gump. It's a prison slang name for homosexuals. Unless you want to be associated with homosexuality, and I wouldn't advice that in prison unless you are one, I would stay away from the homosexual inmates. I know how that sounds but you have got to realize that this is prison that we are talking about. There are no rules for proper etiquette. You may have no feelings one way or the other about homosexuals, but in prison, unless you are a known homosexual, or are seeking them out, you don't want to be associated with them. If you are a homosexual I would use caution about letting anyone else know it. In fact I wouldn't let anyone know it. Homosexual inmates attract inmates looking for sex, any kind of sex. You should tell your Counselor that you are a homosexual as soon as you arrive.

This following is advice from an inmate who has served time at every level of security institution, from penitentiaries to camps.

Being a homosexual in prison is sometimes a type of hustle. Inmates will sell their bodies for money. If an inmate makes someone believe that he is homosexual, regardless if he is or isn't, he will attract those inmates who are looking for sex. An inmate will sometimes be raped because the other inmates think he is a homosexual. A rape is also sometimes used as a form of punishment for non-payment. If you borrow or buy something from another inmate, pay your debt when you agree to.

Movies & Music

Most Federal Institutions will show rented movies on weekends and holidays. These are what are called "Institutional Movies". These movies are usually new release movies that are rented from a local Blockbuster, or other movie rental store. All movies rented are rated "G" or "PG-13". No "R" rated movies shall be shown.

Movies will be broadcast over the units TV's in the TV Rooms. Some of the larger institutions may even have small viewing theaters. Movies will run on Fridays, Saturdays, and holidays. The movies will usually begin after dinner on Fridays. Unless it's a holiday weekend, no movies shall be shown on Sundays.

The following is an example of a movie schedule from September 24, 2004. At the time most of these movies were new releases.

Friday	**10-1-04**	**Intolerable Cruelty**	**1hr 40 min**
Saturday	**10-2-04**	**Lord of the Rings III**	**2hr 30 min**
Friday	**10-8-04**	**Radio**	**1hr 49min**
Saturday	**10-9-04**	**S.W.A.T.**	**1hr 45min**
Holiday	**10-10-04**	**Along Came Polly**	**1hr 30min**
Friday	**10-15-04**	**Paycheck**	**1hr 59min**
Saturday	**10-16-04**	**Star Wars Episode II**	**2hr 20min**
Friday	**10-22-04**	**Seabiscuit**	**2hr 20min**
Saturday	**10-23-04**	**Something's Gotta Give**	**2hr 30min**
Friday	**10-29-04**	**Against The Ropes**	**1hr 49min**

Saturday 10-30-04 Girl Next Door 1hr 49min

****Alternatives: 50 First Dates, Medallion, Haunted Mansion**

****If the schedule movie is not available, one of the alternative movies will be shown in its place.**

NOTE: Regularly scheduled viewing times for TV Programming remains in effect.

At some of the larger camps, and at most lows, there will be music rooms. The BOP will purchase music CD's for inmates to sit and listen to with headphones. The CD's are not allowed to be checked out by the inmates, and will remain in the room. There will be a surprisingly large selection to choose from, with new release titles being added regularly, and almost all music formats available. All music selections will usually be the "PG" rated type, but there may be a few selections with adult lyrics.

At most institutions the Recreation Department will have a FM frequency low band music channel. This is to play CD music that the inmates can listen to with their personal radios. The station will rotate music formats daily and inmates will be allowed to request specific CD's to listen to.

Haircuts

The Barbershop is usually opened Monday – Friday. Most prison barbers are quite good at cutting hair and are provided with scissors and clippers to do the job.

The institution will usually have a Black, White and Hispanic inmate for barbers.

Most inmates will always have freshly cut hair. The inmate barbers get paid by the institution, but most inmates (not all) will pay them anywhere from 6 stamps to a six-pack of soda for a haircut.

Expect very long lines for a haircut especially closer to the weekends.

Some inmates, who are not Institution Barbers, will cut other inmate's hair with clippers that they purchased from the Commissary. This is against policy and could get you thrown in the Hole for doing so.

Toilets & Showers

The toilets in most institutions will be what you probably expect, several stalls with cheap toilet paper and a few urinals. Some institution's toilets will have walls and doors for privacy while others may only have a small partition to separate them. Either way, you can expect them to be busy and constantly in need of cleaning. When using the toilet, you better flush often or you will hear about it.

The showers at most institutions will be the small stalls, like the type that you will find in most health clubs. Other institutions will have the open showers that provide no privacy. The advice I received from a seasoned inmate, who has served time at both state and federal joints, concerning open showers, is to stay as close to the front entrance as possible.

Most Federal Institutions will have the small stalls with shower curtains. Expect to stand in line for a shower, especially in the early evening. If you are in the Hole, your shower will probably be in a shower cell. These are single cells with showers that have a locked iron bar door. Prison showers are also constantly in need of cleaning.

Remember; don't walk to and from the showers in your underwear (panties). Wear your sweats, shorts, or pants on trips to the showers and back to your house.

If you shave in the sinks, clean up the beard stubble after you are finished.

Remember to collect all of your shower, shaving, and clothing items after you are finished. Don't forget something and expect it to be there when you go back to look for it.

Don't be caught in the shower during a count. If your celly is taking a shower and a count is called, you should go and yell at him to get out of the shower to be counted.

Diesel Therapy

When an inmate gets placed in transit, and has to travel in a van or bus for several hundred miles, it is called Diesel Therapy. Some inmates have gone across the country in buses, stopping at county jails along the way for a few weeks at a time. It's the BOP's way of giving an inmate some special time to think about his situation.

Tips & Advice From Other Inmates

The following Notes, Tips, and Advice for new inmates come from some of the many inmates who I served time with. It's written in their own words.

Be yourself. Don't act like you are something that you are not just to try and impress the other inmates. They will see right through you.

Inmates stay informed about current events. They watch the news shows on CNN, Fox, NBC, etc. They also read The Wall Street Journal, Newsweek, Time, etc. Don't think you are smarter than everyone else.

Wash your hands constantly. This will help to prevent illness.

If you are walking through a holdover facility, don't get to close to the cells of inmates who are living there. They aren't going anywhere and may grab you as you walk past just because you are.

Always say this at the end of the day. "Another Day Out Of The Way"

Routine - Do things just to pass time. Regardless if it's, reading, exercising, walking, etc., get into a routine and do it everyday.

Live day-to-day or week-to-week. The whole sentence is too much to deal with.

Sleeping during a stand-up count will get you thrown in the hole.

Locker Space Management. You only have limited space to store your things. Shop smart.

Institutional needs override everything.

Inmates watch you. Wash your hands after using the toilet or you will get labeled as being a filthy pig.

During count time watch both doors. CO's may come in either door to count. You don't want to get caught doing something because they walked through the back door when you were expecting them to come through the front door.

Unit inspections are usually once a week.

The entire unit will be riding you or ignoring you if they think you are “Hot” (a snitch).

Take the good with the bad. At least you are not at the next higher-level institution. The higher you go, the worse they get.

Bed Bugs, get use to them.

Anyone can trip-up and go to prison.

Camp maybe boring, but at least you can come and go.

Being locked down, like behind the fence, is even more boring.

Camp isn’t what it use to be since 60 Minutes did the show on Club Fed.

Inmate Cooking. You will learn how to make some really good dishes.

Waiting for showers, get use to it.

Inmates that sit around talking about how when they get out they are going to do the same thing again that they got busted for is just amazing.

Behind the fence you got more staff watching you during meals. You are supposed to have access to talk to them (counselors) but they don't want you to.

NASCAR fans vs. NBA fans - TV Viewing Wars

NASCAR races will be watched or there will be a lot of crying and complaining.

Don't be a "Mooch". Save your money and buy your own stuff.

New menu items at commissary - creates a buzz in the air.

Trash cans in cell or cube needs to be washed out each week.

Read as much as you can to pass time.

Magazine subscriptions can be ordered cheaply through Tightwad Magazines. Have someone look them up on the Internet.

Running out of telephone minutes. You only get 300 a month, use them wisely.

Everything the CO asks for is needed immediately!

Listen for CO's radio in the unit. It will alert you to their presence.

New fish get the worst bedding.

Standing in line, get use to it.

Don't call another inmate out unless you plan on fighting.

Earplugs - maintenance and landscape workers will have them.

Envelopes folded over desk lights will dim the light enough to allow your cellie to sleep.

Snoring, get use to it.

On your day off, you could still be called to work. Institutional needs.

Behind the fence TV's off at midnight, weekends at 2:00 a.m. unless you have a cool CO during night counts who doesn't care. Most inmates watch through the windows at other units. If they see the TV's going off they turn theirs off and go to their house until after the count. Then they go back to watching TV.

Don't fall asleep watching TV at night.

No visiting other units.

Don't keep saying how useless this place is or how big a waste of taxpayer's money this place is. Other inmates get tired of hearing anything that gets said too much.

Don't constantly complain. No one likes a whiner.

Behind the fence, at 8:30 p.m. the Rec. Yard gets closed for the night.

Behind the fence, unit doors get locked at the end of the 10-minute move. Get to where you are going during the move.

Five-foot space next to a fence. Sign says do not cross, DO NOT CROSS IT!

Yelling out inmate's names at their unit's door to see if they are in there is annoying as hell.

Electric fan, if your joint sells them, buy one. You will be glad you did in the summer.

Ear Hustling. Don't listen to other's conversations.

The CO's rotate quarterly. Sometimes you get good ones and sometimes you get assholes.

Mackerel can top folded over is used for cutting up vegetables when you cook.

Inmates who walk-away from camp are dumb-asses! It doesn't get any easier than camp.

Holiday tournaments - pool, cards, chess. Win food prizes.

The telephone is great, but mail is important also.

Going home is a nervous time for inmates.

Use the toilets after the orderly has cleaned them. You will be glad you did.

CO's are also called Police, Jake, The Po Po, and One Time.

If an inmate tells you something about themselves do not repeat it to anyone else - this is a trust issue.

A lot of wagers are bet for push-ups.

Driver's license - bring it with you if possible. You may get some type of driving job if you have a current driver's license.

Escape by death. What it's called when an inmate dies in custody.

Packed out - CO's collect your things from your cube when you get thrown in the Hole.

At state joints fighting is almost expected. Programs help you get parole in state joints - Anger Management, A.A., Drug Programs, Repress Stress

Jiggy Fly, Dre, Snoop, Smokey, Q. Are all Nicknames, have one when you get here or you will get hung with one that you might not like?

Food - sometimes just grits and a muffin for breakfast.

Camp is somewhat difficult until you adjust then it's just a joke on the taxpayers.

Going to prison today carries the same stigma that single mothers and filing bankruptcy did in the past. It's just not as big a deal as it once was.

You, a relative, or someone you know will go to prison in your lifetime.

Work in maintenance and learn enough skills to start your own biz when you get released.

Better yourself while you are here. Stay positive. Lots of people richer, famous and better then you have gone to prison.

Radio stations - you will get a different mix, if you are lucky.

Toilet paper, keep a few rolls in your cube just incase.

Buy hangers for your uniforms.

Inmates will wager on anything, including American Idol and Survivor.

You can be anything you want in prison by fronting (acting and talking like you are something else other than who you really are).

Younger guys take the TV Room over. Older inmates hardly get to watch TV.

A view from your yard is nice if you have it. Even a few trees are something to look at.

Don't ear hustle! If one inmate asks another what 1 + 1 is and he doesn't know, don't butt into their conversation and give the answer. Mind your own business! Always!

Buy an extra laundry bag from the commissary and keep clean clothes folded in it. It will free up locker space.

Rapping knuckles on table in cafeteria when you get up to leave is a sign of respect.

Unit water fountains usually have a hot water supply to make coffee, soup, and hot chocolate with.

Eat low fat.

Being in TV rooms for accountability (a count). Sometimes yes, sometimes no.

Copouts are for issues, problems, and requests that you turn into the Counselor or anyone on the staff that you wish to talk to.

Cooking. You will be cooking a lot of chicken, tuna, mackerel and rice.

Shakedowns and walk-through inspections happen a lot.

Different wardens have different rules.

No visits by convicted felons, even if it's your wife.

New COs brings new routines.

Inmate "millionaires" who are in the GED class. What a joke!

Behind the fence the telephone are in the units. Usually 2 phones in each unit.

A lot of inmates' suntan in the spring and summer.

Custody, Care, and Control. This is the BOP's motto.

An SIS investigation could keep you in the hole for 90 days.

Inmates walk around trying to sell you food, like homemade banana pudding and peanut butter fudge.

Pull your bunk bed out from the wall when changing bedding or making up the bed. Is much easier than standing on a stool.

Use your items to their last drop - soap, shampoo, and deodorant.

Season change causes inmates tempers to flare up.

Keep eye on laundry, it may walk off.

Being in transit to go back to court sucks. You probably will have to go through Atlanta and that place is the worse holdover facility in the BOP.

Only allowed to have 5 books in your possession at any one time.

Do laundry early in the a.m., if possible. No line.

Participate in team or league sports. Basketball, softball, volleyball, etc.

Visits keep your spirits up.

You have to wear uniforms to breakfast & lunch but usually not to dinner Monday - Friday. Weekends & holidays you don't have to wear uniforms at any meals.

Watching the news and reading newspapers keeps you attached to the world outside. Some inmates would rather not stay attached.

You will get a better understanding of why child molesters and rapists get treated so harshly by other inmates when you see a story on the news and start thinking about how you aren't at home to protect your loved ones.

Keep clean - you will be talked about.

Your day's activities revolve around counts and, if behind the fence, 10 minute moves.

If you only have 12 - 24 months to do, don't whine, you will get no sympathy. That is considered to be short time and a vacation by most inmates.

Commissary day - inmates everywhere are looking for pigeons (someone who will buy them something)

No lying in bed, made or not, during work call hours if behind the fence. The CO will find you something to do. At camp most of the CO's could care less if you lay on your bunk as long as it is made.

Don't confuse someone's intelligence with the way he speaks.

This isn't high school. If you see fights don't try and break them up. Mind your own business.

Merry-go-round paperwork - going home paperwork that you have to get different CO's to sign.

Most inmates give their things away when going home.

Skid row beds are beds that are placed in hallways or stairwells because there are no cubes or cells available.

If no weights - do imaginative workouts - dips, squats, weighted laundry bags.

Inspections will always find something wrong. The staff believes inmates need goals to set and that they should attempt to reach them. They are full of crap.

After reading a new magazine or book, pass it on for others to read.

Birthday parties and going home parties are all about eating food.

Out-count workers - Usually food service workers who are working in the cafeteria during count time.

Using someone else's Inmate ID for anything is a shot and the Hole.

Medical sick call - comical!

Dentist. They believe pulling teeth is the cheapest and easiest way to deal with inmate's teeth.

Different types of counts. Holiday, Weekend Counts, Photo Counts, Fog Counts, Emergency Counts, Special Counts, Knuckle Counts, Middle of the Night Counts, Stand-Up Counts, and Accountability Counts.

Arguments between players and referees, during basketball league play, are comical.

Breath analyzer tests and urine tests are given without warnings.

Go to the hole get hit on mattress & pillow (other inmates will take your bedding when you go to the Hole) unless your cellie holds them down for you.

Transfer furloughs to other camps - Warden decides.

If you are in the Hole on visiting day your visitors will be turned away.

Pest control sheet. Get your house sprayed as often as possible.

Visits, at first you may not want them but you will soon wish you had them.

Isolation unit is for gang-bangers, violence, and investigations. It's also for protective custody.

Copout for the dentist, expect a wait of 4-6 months for cleaning and at least a year for needed work.

Food theft happens. Watch your food.

At higher security joints walk with back to wall as much as possible.

Locks and socks. When someone places their combination lock into a sock and swings it as a weapon.

Mind your business, don't rat, don't look like you have money and you will be ok.

Watch out for inmates who want to get to know you, to see what you are about.

Miss your Call-Out and receive a shot and/or a trip to the Hole.

Read the Call-Out Board everyday.

Some rats snitch just to snitch. They get no reward.

Weight Training. If you need help, and can afford it, hire an inmate personal trainer to help you get into shape.

Riding in a car means that you are in a group that works out together. Driving the car means that you're in charge and are deciding what exercise the group will be doing.

"One Dip - No Lip" is the motto of Food Service CO's.

Grip-Up means putting on boots or shoes if you are planning to be in a fight.

Ultra Light for Hands - is a contraband nickname

Live on the basics that the BOP provides as much as possible.

Jack the Rec. Means that you are trying to get out of working out, or you are wasting time in the weight room.

Tickets - shots.

Gump - Homosexual.

Chairs get saved after the 4:00 p.m. count for the evening TV viewing.

Chairs are often saved using a towel, cup or radio and headphones.

Don't move TV chairs around after they have been saved. Respect others.

Other inmates sometimes loan new inmates old shower shoes and a radio. They expect you to get your own as soon as possible.

Mail - Love from home.

It's easy to make enemies and its easy not to.

Car jacking in the weight room. When an inmate in a car who is not driving is trying to decide what exercises the group will do.

Leave the toilet and shower in the condition that you would want to find them in.

Give way when walking narrow walkways try not to bump shoulders unless you are just a mean son-of-a-bitch.

If you are not healthy when your release date finally rolls around, you might have to stay longer.

State inmates usually wear blue uniforms.

Green uniform for camps.

Beige uniform for inmates behind the fence (low, med. & penitentiaries).

Orange worn for transport, detention, & death row.

Getting hit - getting a shot.

Get loose fitting uniforms when you arrive.

Wear underwear when self-surrendering or you will be talked about.

Female visitors should carry a clear plastic bag instead of a purse.

No purses, books, cards, diaper bags, bottles, phones, pagers, or meds (except nitro pills) are allowed in the visiting room. Let your people who plan on visiting know this. There is a list of what is allowed that you can mail them.

Photos are taken in the visiting room for $1.00 a piece.

Knock Rocks (lightly punching each others fists) with other inmates instead of shaking hands.

Basketball court is sometimes called the jungle.

Don't sit on other inmate's beds or desks.

Phones turned off for 30 minutes after counts.

Mail Call. It sometimes is ok for others to get your mail for you, except legal mail.

Every 9 months you can exchange your whites at the laundry.

Lots of fruit fly's get on your fruit in prison.

Alarm clocks. Don't set them and not be there when they go off.

Just because they don't call count doesn't mean they are not counting, be aware of count time.

Tell your family and friends, "If you say you are going to visit then visit. Don't have me get cleaned up and dressed then not show up."

Tell your family and friends, "Don't lie and say you sent something to me in the mail when you didn't. I'll know."

Richie Rich - inmate with money.

Take advantage of library and exercise; stay sharp in mind and body.

TV's sometimes get removed as punishment.

Always show Warden his respect even if you don't mean it. He will throw your ass in the Hole if he thinks he is not getting his respect.

Thorazine Shuffle - Inmates walking after they have had their meds.

Gambling on football and basketball tickets is just Rec.

Briefs (underwear) "Panties", "Tighty Whities" - sometimes called "Catch Me F*** Me Drawers"

PV - parole violator.

Unit Orderlies - hope you have good ones that do a good job cleaning the toilets and showers.

Write your name on your things with a marker in large letters.

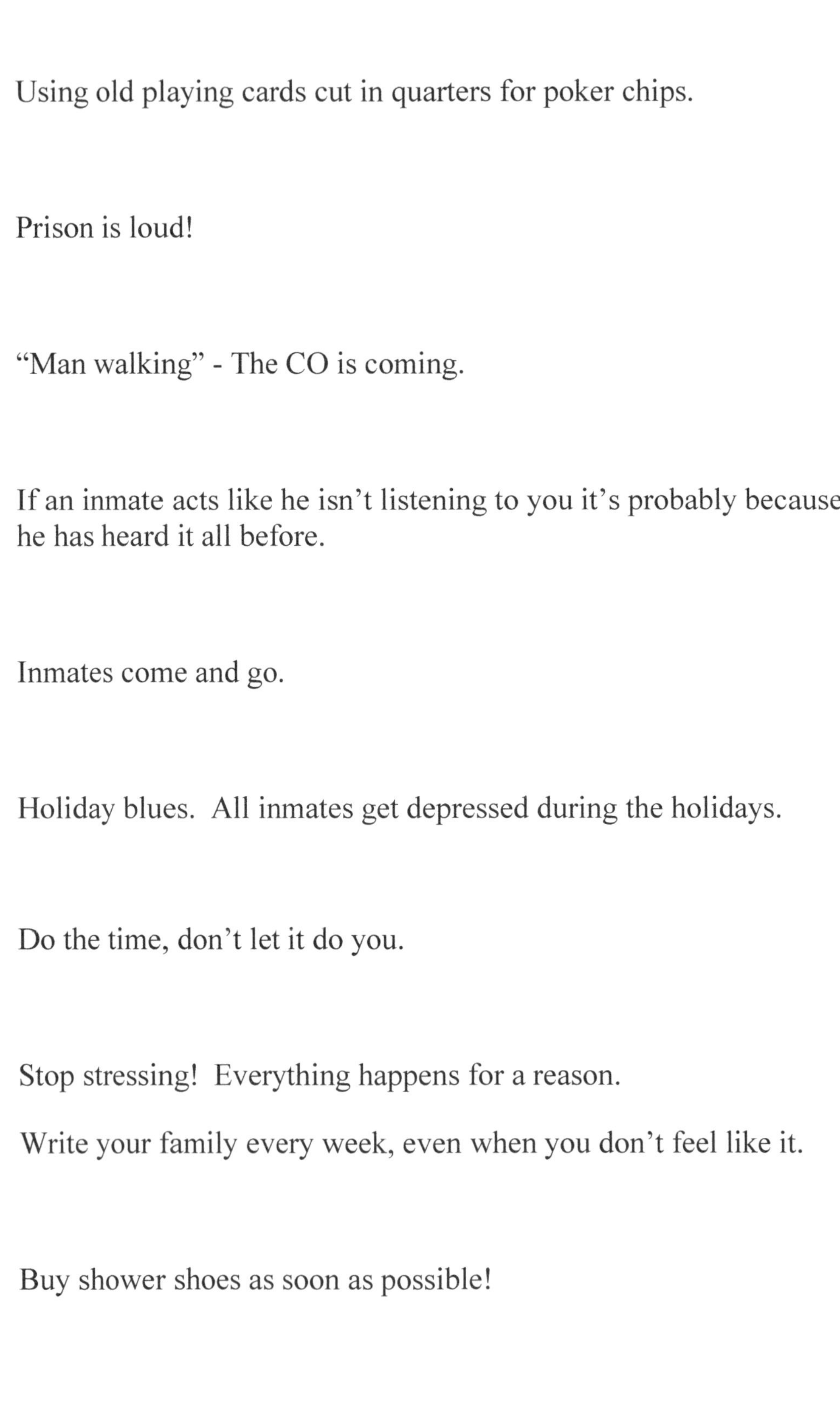

Using old playing cards cut in quarters for poker chips.

Prison is loud!

"Man walking" - The CO is coming.

If an inmate acts like he isn't listening to you it's probably because he has heard it all before.

Inmates come and go.

Holiday blues. All inmates get depressed during the holidays.

Do the time, don't let it do you.

Stop stressing! Everything happens for a reason.

Write your family every week, even when you don't feel like it.

Buy shower shoes as soon as possible!

Don't gamble too much.

Tightwad Magazines will allow you to subscribe to certain magazines for stamps as payment.

Eat what they give you, but always ask others if they want it, before you throw any food away.

Get use to instant coffee.

If you play a musical instrument, let someone know. Prison has some of the best musicians going as inmates and they usually have a band that plays for the other inmates.

If you get sick go to medical. Colds and viruses spread like wildfire in the units. Keep your cold to yourself.

God's love is always present, even here.

Half Way House

Most all inmates, upon release, will have to spend a period of time in a Half Way House. The following (taken from the BOP's website) is the description of the Half Way House program that the BOP and most states utilize.

Community corrections is an integral component of the Bureau's correctional programs. Community corrections staff develop and administer contracts for community-based correctional programs and serve as the Bureau's local liaison with the Federal courts, the U.S. Marshals Service, state and local corrections, and a variety of community groups. Through the community corrections program, the Bureau has also developed agreements with state and local governments and contracts with privately operated facilities for the confinement of federally adjudicated juveniles and for the detention or secure confinement of some Federal inmates.

The Bureau's community-based programs are administered by staff of the Correctional Programs Division in Central Office (in Washington, DC), community corrections regional management teams in each of the Bureau's six regional offices, and the employees of 28 community corrections management (CCM) field offices serving specific judicial districts within their regions.

The Bureau contracts with residential re-entry centers (RRCs), also known as **halfway houses**, to provide assistance to inmates who are nearing release. RRCs provide a safe, structured, supervised environment, as well as employment counseling, job placement, financial management assistance, and other programs and services. RRCs help inmates gradually rebuild their ties to the community and facilitate supervising offenders' activities during this readjustment phase. An important component of the RRC program is transitional drug abuse treatment for inmates who have completed residential substance abuse treatment program while confined in a Bureau institution.

RRC Placement

Accountability. Inmates participating in release programming at a RRC remain in Federal custody while serving a sentence imposed by the U.S. District Court. Accordingly, RRC staff monitor an inmate's location and movement 24 hours/day. The contractor authorizes an inmate to leave the RRC through sign-out procedures for approved activities, such as seeking employment, working, counseling, visiting, or recreation. Staff continues to monitor inmates by visiting the approved locations (home or work) and/or making random phone contacts at different times during the day. Staff also administers random drug and alcohol tests for those inmates returning to the RRC from an approved activity and conduct random in-house counts throughout the day.

Employment. Ordinarily, all offenders are expected to be employed 40 hours/week within 15 calendar days after their arrival at the RRC. Staff is available at the RRC to assist inmates in obtaining employment through a network of local employers, employment job fairs, and training classes in resume writing, interview techniques, etc.

Housing. During their stay, inmates are required to pay a subsistence fee to help defray the cost of their confinement; this charge is 25 percent of their gross income, not to exceed the average daily cost of their RRC placement. The contractor assists inmates in locating suitable housing (if necessary), to which they can release from the RRC. In cases where an inmate will be released with supervision, the contractor verifies the proposed address and forwards their comments to the U.S. Probation Office.

Substance Abuse Treatment/Counseling. All RRCs offer drug testing and counseling for alcohol and drug-related problems. Contractors provide treatment and/or counseling based upon the offender's needs and substance abuse history. Counseling may be performed at the RRC with qualified staff, while treatment may be provided through a contract between the Bureau's Transitional Drug Abuse Treatment (TDAT) program and certified treatment providers.

Medical/Mental Health Treatment. Ordinarily, inmates are expected to be responsible for their own medical expenses while residing in a RRC. Contractors usually maintain a network of social service agencies to assist inmates, if the need arises during transition. In an emergency and on a case-by-case basis, the contractor is responsible for obtaining the necessary treatment required to preserve the inmate's life. The Bureau provides a 30-day supply of medication to cover the first 30 days of an inmate's stay at a RRC (under limited circumstances, more may be provided).

Comprehensive Sanction Centers (CSCs)

Initiated by the Bureau with the extensive collaboration from U.S. Probation and contractors, the CSC concept was created to facilitate the development and implementation of individualized community program plans tailored to offenders' specific needs. Approximately 45 percent of Federal inmates in community-based programs are housed in CSCs. While similar to RRCs, CSCs offer a more structured system for granting inmates gradual access to the community: for example, CSCs have five levels of supervision, ranging from 24-hour confinement to home confinement.

CSCs also require that inmates participate in more programs. They may include an intensive treatment component consisting of substance abuse education, life skills training, mental health counseling, education, employment assistance, and monitoring. A Program Review Team (PRT) systematically reviews the inmate's progress, with representatives from the Bureau, U.S. Probation, and the contractor. The U.S. Probation Office is also formally involved in the release planning process.

Home Confinement

Some Federal inmates are placed on home confinement for a brief period at the end of their prison term. Home confinement is a generic term used to cover all circumstances under which an inmate is required to remain at home during non-working hours of the day. They serve this portion of their sentences at home under strict schedules and curfew requirements. Electronic monitoring equipment is sometimes used to monitor compliance with the program's conditions. This program provides an opportunity for inmates to assume increasing levels of responsibility, while, at the same time, providing sufficient restrictions to promote community safety and convey the sanctioning value of the sentence. Statutory provisions limit the length of home confinement to the last 6 months or 10 percent of the sentence, whichever is less. Ordinarily, an inmate is placed in a RRC or CSC prior to placement on home confinement.

Final Thoughts

This brings us to the end of our guidebook. We hope you found it to be informative, and that you will benefit from reading it.

When a person is incarcerated at a prison or prison camp, it changes the way he looks at the world. Some inmates get meaner, and have a harder take on life. Some become born again Christians who turn to God for answers. Some inmates vow to change the way they have been living their lives, and to become better husbands and fathers. You too will experience some type of change. Hopefully it will be for the better.

Although every inmate wants to be released as soon as possible, most get very nervous when that day finally rolls around. Many inmates don't have homes to return to, and some have no family. Most of them don't have a clue as to where they will live or work.

Bureau of Justice Statistics show that as of 2001, nearly 70 percent of all released prisoners will be rearrested within three years. This is called Recidivism. When you are released you will discover that there is no support system waiting for you. A survey taken in several larger cities found that 65 percent of employers would not knowingly hire an ex-convict. I believe that this is one reason the Recidivism rate is so high. Many inmates believe it's better to be locked up and to be taken care of, than to be free, unemployed, and homeless.

It's these reasons that I encourage you to take every opportunity to better yourself during your period of incarceration. Read, exercise, and learn a trade in maintenance. Then, once you are released, you can start your own business and work for yourself, or how about writing a book?

Remember, time turns even while you are in prison. It's the one thing that the government has no control over! Do your time well, and benefit from the exercise and educational growth that you will have the chance to experience. Stay calm and don't stress about anything that you cannot change. Remember the Inmate's 10 Commandments, avoid the 8 Sins, and you will be okay.

Good luck & God bless.

CPSIA information can be obtained at www.ICGtesting.com
Printed in the USA
LVOW011541090512

281029LV00001B/95/P